W9-BCK-816

TRAINING
RETRIEVERS
FOR
Marshes and Meadows

TRAINING
RETRIEVERS
FOR
Marshes and Meadows

James B. Spencer

Alpine
PUBLICATIONS

Loveland, Colorado

Copyright © 1998, 1990, by James B. Spencer
All rights reserved. No part of this book may be used or
reproduced in any manner whatsoever without written permission
from the publisher, except in the case of brief quotations embodied
in critical reviews. For permission, write to Alpine Publications, Inc.,
P. O. Box 7027, Loveland, CO 80537.

Library of Congress Cataloging in Publication Data
Spencer, James B.
Training retrievers for the marshes and meadows/James B.
Spencer.—2nd ed.
p.   cm.
Includes index.
ISBN 1-57779-007-3
I. Title
SF429.R4S64   1998
636.752'735—dc21
97-48314 CIP

This book is available at special quantity discounts
for breeders and for club promotions, premiums,
or educational use. Write for details.

1 2 3 4 5 6 7 8 9 0

Cover Photo: Dr. John Shannon
Text photos by the author except as noted.
Book design by Rudy J. Ramos, Ramos Design Studio
Printed in the United States of America.

*To Duffy and Brandy, two Golden Retrievers
that taught me more, gave me more, and
forgave me more than I did them.*

Contents

PREFACE, *ix*

CHAPTER ONE
An Overview, *1*

CHAPTER TWO
Puppy Training, *15*

CHAPTER THREE
Basic ObedienceTraining, *37*

CHAPTER FOUR
Single Marked Retrieves, *71*

CHAPTER FIVE
Force-Breaking, *99*

CHAPTER SIX
Double Marked Retrieves, *129*

CHAPTER SEVEN
Basic Blind Retrieve Training—In Pieces, *157*

CHAPTER EIGHT
Advanced Marks and Blinds, *193*

CHAPTER NINE
Yours Will Be a Great Retriever All Too Soon, *219*

INDEX, *225*

Preface

The amateur, even the beginner with his first dog, has advantages over the professional retriever trainer, just as the pro has advantages over the amateur. The difference is that the pros make the most of theirs, while most amateurs fail to recognize that they have advantages, too.

The pro has proper facilities and equipment: large land and water areas for retriever training; bird pens stocked with pigeons, ducks, and pheasants; extensive kennel space; a truck designed for transporting dogs; full-time assistants; training tools from nineteenth century buggy-whips to hi-tech electronic collars.

The amateur has advantages, too; for example, rapport . . . his pup will follow him anywhere. *Photo by Theresa Spencer.*

The pro has time. D. L. Walters, for example, works his retrievers all morning and all afternoon, seven days a week, eleven months a year. He takes the entire month of December off, sends all the dogs back to their owners, and says, "I don't even want to see a dog while I'm hunting." Comes January 1 and he is charged up and anxious to start training again. He has been doing this for over forty years, and still shows excitement when the dogs return.

The pro has knowledge gained through experience. He trains more dogs in a year than most amateurs do in a lifetime. He normally has twenty to forty dogs in his runs at any given time. Some of them, especially the field trial dogs, are "lifers," dogs that spend their entire active lives in his kennels. Others, those with a particular problem, are in and out.

The pro has a "program." To the casual observer, it looks like an assembly line. Untrained dogs go in one end, pass through a series of stations, and come out the other end as finished retrievers. Even the wash-outs look like partially completed products that failed in inspection. Actually, the program is much more personal than that, for pros are dog-lovers first and trainers second. Most of them could make a better living in another line of work.

However, the pro also has pressures. Clients want to see near-miraculous progress every time they drop in, and they normally do that once or twice a month. If the pro does field trials or hunting tests, his clients expect frequent successes—and the sooner the better. Field trials, being competitive, become tougher and tougher every year, so success becomes more and more demanding.

To keep the close kin in cider and sow-belly, the pro must cram more training into less time with each new dog that comes on the place. He has no choice. The combination of demanding owners and the growing complexity of field trials puts him in a vise. Even the pros who do hunting tests exclusively feel some of that squeeze, for there is a trickle-down from field trials to hunting tests (whether the sponsors of the latter wish to admit it or not).

Thus, the pro's program accelerates each year. "Inspections" become more rigorous. Retrievers that cannot keep up are washed out. After all, it's to the pro's advantage to steer each owner towards a dog that can make it through his program on schedule, rather than try to explain away any lack of progress. It's like a high-stake game of five-card stud, where the smart players immediately fold anything less than a wired pair or a high hole-card. They know they will go broke sticking around waiting for a late-developing hand, like a flush or a straight.

Retriever training is conditioning. You can't sit down and explain to the animal what you want him to do and not do. No, you have to condition him with rewards and punishments. Conditioning with rewards is slow. Conditioning with punishment is fast—and traumatic.

Thus, the more accelerated the program, the more traumatic it becomes for the dog. Pros don't like it, but what choice do they have, given that they are training retrievers for a living in an environment that dictates speed or starvation?

The cruelest irony of this situation is that many amateurs learn their training techniques from pros. On the surface, that makes sense. The pros have facilities, knowledge, and a program. However, the amateur has advantages any pro would love to have.

Most important, the amateur has flow-time. The pro may have more training hours per day and more training days per year, but the amateur has more assured training flow-time per dog. No one will take the dog away from the amateur if the animal doesn't keep up with an arbitrary (and sporty) schedule. No, the amateur can train according to the dog's built-in schedule. If the dog doesn't take immediately to birds, he can give him more time. If force-breaking takes a couple of months, so what? And so on.

His flow-time advantage allows the amateur to condition his dog with praise more than with punishment. He can lead the animal through the process, praise him for success, over and over until it becomes a habit. Then, he can allow the dog to make the normal mistakes and punish him for them. The pooch will understand what he did wrong, how to avoid future punishment.

I have a saying for this kind of training: Trial-and-success teaches; trial-and-error only reinforces what has already been taught.

His flow-time advantage also allows the amateur to train more gradually. He doesn't have to extend the dog to the maximum distance in every mark, every blind retrieve, in the shortest possible time. He can let the dog experience success through small incremental increases in distance.

I have a saying for that, too: A short success is better than a long failure.

The amateur has another advantage in the rapport he has with his individual retriever. The amateur may not be able to train as many hours a year, but he can buddy around with his dog more than the pro can. He can also start earlier, when he first brings the pup home. The pup forms stronger attachments then than at any later time in his life.

That rapport makes the amateur's praise more rewarding and his punishment more painful. Thus, he doesn't have to be as rough with his dog as a pro would to get the same response.

The amateur also has an option not available to the pro when a minor problem comes up in training: He can decide to live with whatever quirk the dog exhibits rather than train through it. Over the years I have overlooked any number of little peculiarities that a pro would have to overcome. Duffy lifted his leg on the return of almost every retrieve he ever made. Field trial judge Darrell Kincaid once asked me if I rented Duffy out to the fire department between trials (and then added he would gladly buy him). Brandy danced around at the line like a circus dog.

In this book, I present a program which allows the amateur to use his advantages. This is a gentle program, based primarily on praise and positive motivation.

However, it is not a sweetness-and-light program in which the dog is never punished. No, dog training is conditioning, and conditioning demands both praise for proper behavior and punishment for improper behavior. I have never trained a dog without punishment, and neither will you.

I must admit that I have never trained a dog without inappropriate punishment, punishment in anger. I am not a patient person. In fact, my wife says that I still have all the patience I was born with—because I have never used any of it.

I remember blowing my stack at Belle, a golden, one evening and frightening her so badly that she jumped in the nearest lake and swam in circles where I couldn't reach her. As I stood on shore pondering whether to shed some clothing and go after her, a fellow retrieverite came over and said, "You know, I read an article in GUN DOG about how to handle this problem. It's in the current issue, as a matter of fact. You ought to read it." Then he looked knowingly at me and chuckled. I had written the article, of course, and was doing exactly the opposite of everything I had recommended to my readers. I broke out laughing, sat down to wait for Belle. She eventually came ashore, slunk over to me, and placed her head in my lap. We started over again, with better results.

Yeah, I make mistakes like that. However, I recognize them as mistakes, not as part of the program. I think about every one of them later, regret it, even go out to the offended dog's run late in the evening to make up. Foolish, I know, for a dog has no way of understanding an apology. I am encouraged that I suffer such contrition less frequently each year. Perhaps age is substituting for patience.

This is also an elastic program, with no fixed schedule. Your retriever has his own built-in maturity rate, his own IQ (if you will), his own likes and dislikes. All of these affect how rapidly you can train him. For each phase of training, I give you the prerequisites. Your youngster should not move into any phase until he has completed all its prerequisites. It doesn't matter when your buddy's dog is ready, or when the author of some book with a machine-gun schedule claimed his dog was ready. Only your individual dog's schedule matters.

Attitude is everything in this gentle, elastic program. You should assume the role of teacher. You must accept full responsibility for success. You must be determined to complete the program, to work as hard and as long as that takes. You must decide to use the techniques that work for your individual dog at the times they work. You must praise when that aids the learning process, which is most of the time, especially in the early stages of every phase of training. You must punish only when that aids learning. In other words, when the dog needs it, not when you feel like it.

In puppy training (Chapter Two), you establish rapport, and you become a secondary "lair" for your pup.

In Basic Obedience (Chapter Three), you build obedience on freedom, much as we in this country have built a law-abiding society on individual freedom.

In Single Marked Retrieves (Chapter Four) and Double Marked Retrieves (Chapter Six), you do all your initial work on bare ground, where failure is impossible. Trial-and-success.

In Blind Retrieve Training (Chapter Seven), you help your dog use "pictures" to give him something to run to, instead of giving him punishment to run from.

However, the difference between this program and the professional program is most dramatically apparent in Chapter 5,

Force-Breaking. Force-breaking has a bad reputation in retriever circles because of the quick-and-rough "Hell Week" technique most pros use (by economic necessity, not by choice). The technique I present is slow and gentle, and as effective as Hell Week.

In 1983 I did a two-parter, titled "Force-Breaking: Nonsense or Necessity?" for RETRIEVER INTERNATIONAL magazine. First I had to convince publisher/editor Maryanne Foote that I would describe a technique that wouldn't offend her most delicate reader. After it was published, she received all sorts of positive responses from subscribers. It was nominated by Dog Writers Association of America (DWAA) in the Best Series category in its 1983 writing contest. That two-parter has been reprinted in the newsletters of the following national breed clubs: Golden Retriever Club of America, Golden Retriever Club of Canada, Flat-Coated Retriever Society of America, Curly-Coated Retriever Club of America. It has also been reprinted in the newsletters of several local and regional retriever field trial clubs in this country and Canada.

In 1987 I did a three-parter, titled "Force-Breaking," for GUN DOG. Here too the publisher, Carrell Bunn, was initially reluctant to touch such a subject. Again, DWAA nominated it, this time in the Best Column category. During the time this series was being published, I received a number of SOS phone calls and letters requesting the parts that had not yet been published. I have received numerous requests for reprints. Many have written to express gratitude for this series ever since it was published. As a matter of fact, I received a very flattering letter just yesterday, fully a year and a half after the third part was published.

One of my motives in writing this book has been to present this gentle force-breaking technique in a more permanent form.

Another motive has been to help the beginner form good handling habits. Ben Hogan once said that if a person would, on first picking up a golf club, do exactly the opposite of what every instinct dictates, he would have a pretty good golf swing. Handling a retriever is not so exotic. However, I have seen beginners make so many mistakes—and such silly mistakes—that they have seriously handicapped their retrievers.

The handler's job is to assist the dog. Anything that promotes good dog work is good handling. Anything that distracts or interferes with the dog is bad handling. Obviously, good handling must be consistent, retrieve after retrieve. In every chapter, I present handling techniques that are helpful and consistent—and not nearly as difficult as swinging a golf club correctly.

I hope as you read this book you discover that you can train your retriever without undue harshness. It may take longer, but who cares? No one will take your dog away from you if you don't stay on a tight schedule. Besides, when you finish, you will still have a lot of dog under all that hair, a dog that shows joy in his work. You won't have to suffer a lifeless machine that does everything precisely, correctly, but without animation and style.

Good luck!

An Overview

WELCOME

I can visualize you sitting there in your most comfortable chair with your young retriever at your side. Before you start reading, you went through your standard ritual. Perhaps you lit the fireplace. You may have poured yourself a martini, a scotch, or a cognac, depending on the season and time of day. You fussed with the pillow in your chair. You sat down and scrunched around a bit. You picked up the book and scrutinized its cover. You glanced through the table of contents, then flipped through to look at a few photos. You closed the book, then jiggled and juggled it gently, just to allow its size and weight to become comfortable in your hands.

> To train a retriever, a person must first dream dreams . . . like this hardy Chesapeake may be doing.

Through that ritual you dreamed of the wonderful things your retriever will one day do. Perhaps you saw him bouncing through the heavy cover along the edge of a cut and snow-powdered grain field, carrying a rooster pheasant with its long tail stretching from one side of his mouth and its iridescent head bobbing from the other. Perhaps you saw him leap far out into the waves of a large impoundment to recover the banded mallard you just dropped from a flock of seven. Perhaps you saw him sitting beside you in a pit blind surrounded by shell goose decoys, with one giant Canada lying at your side as you called to another flock half a mile off. Perhaps you saw him squirming through the tangles with the Ruffed Grouse he flushed and you shot without actually seeing.

I dream those kind of things for my young retrievers, too. Right now, I see Rhett, my young golden...but never mind. You know what I mean.

I also reminisce about days afield with retrievers long dead. Duffy and Brandy especially.

Dreaming about the future differs only slightly from reminiscing about the past. In both, I find birds plentiful and conditions perfect. In both, I never miss a shot, and only cripple a bird now and then to allow my dog to show what he can do. In both, I idealize my dog's performance substantially beyond the probable, sometimes slightly beyond the possible. *And, in both, I find the desire, the energy, the determination necessary to do the day-in-day-out work that training a retriever requires.*

So go ahead and dream about the wonderful things your retriever will do after you get him trained. Enjoy.

As I said, your untrained retriever sits there beside you. It may be any of eight breeds: American water spaniel, Chesapeake, curly-coat, flat-coat, golden, Irish water spaniel, Labrador, or Nova Scotia duck tolling retriever. It may be a just-weaned pup or an older untrained dog. It may be male or female. However, since our language lacks a singular for "they," that is, a third person singular personal pronoun without gender, I will call your retriever "him." No offense. Neither of us wants to struggle through a book full of "he/she's" and "him/her's."

I hope my book, *Hunting Retrievers: Hindsights, Foresights, and Insights* (Alpine, 1989) helped you select both the breed and the individual dog for you. I hope it helped you decide how to house the rascal. Most of all, I hope it enlightened you about the retriever world: national breed clubs, local breed clubs, local field trial and hunting test clubs, field trials, hunting tests, and working certificate tests.

I also hope that before you get to actual field work, you will buy a copy of my book, *Retriever Training Tests* (Alpine Publications, 1997), so you can learn how to set up appropriate tests for your retriever as he progresses through the training program.

YOUR TRAINING PROGRAM
Training Sequence
Training is a continuous process, not a series of disconnected parts or phases (obedience, marked retrieves, blind retrieves, etc.). However, it is not what mathematicians call "linear." By that I mean you do not complete all of one phase before starting the next. Sometimes you work on multiple phases in a single session. Sometimes you work on multiple phases in parallel for a sustained period of time.

I have divided the training program into seven basic parts or phases and devoted a chapter to each: Puppy Training, Basic Obedience Training, Single Marked Retrieves, Force-Breaking, Double Marked Retrieves, Basic Blind Retrieve Training, and Advanced Marks and Blinds. These chapters are arranged so they follow the general sequence of your training. However, you will frequently use training described in two or more chapters in parallel. A few examples: The single mark training in Chapter Four goes on in parallel with the obedience training in Chapter Three; the double mark training in Chapter Six runs in parallel with the blind retrieve training in Chapter Seven.

Don't fret about this. You will find these situations clearly marked.

Besides, once you understand the overall training vehicle, you will understand how all the parts, sub-assemblies, and assemblies must logically fit together. To gain a big-picture view of the program, read the entire book before you apply any of it. Then, when you reread each chapter during the actual training of your retriever, you will understand how that chapter fits into the overall plan.

Your Schedule
At my seminars, too many questions start out, "How long does it take to train a dog to...?" My initial answer never satisfies the questioner: "It takes as long as it takes, like an inning in baseball."

I generally add some reasonable range of times, with qualifying examples. For instance, I tell folks it takes me 3 to 5 weeks to force-break an average retriever. Then, I tell them about spending two and a half months on one, and only two weeks on another. It all depends on how quickly I get that "third out."

Retrievers are not machines. They are sensitive animals. While they lack human intelligence (forcing us to condition them rather than reason with them), they share our emotions. They experience fear; they become bewildered; they feel joy; they love; and they hate. They also have physical traits like ours. They feel invigorated or tired. I'm sure they have headaches and backaches, but they can't complain verbally. They have good days and bad days. Any training program which ignores those emotional and physical characteristics to meet some fanciful schedule will ruin ten dogs for every one it "makes."

Different breeds mature at different rates. The Labrador matures most rapidly, followed by the golden. The flat-coat and toller are a bit slower. Slower still are the Irish water spaniel, American water spaniel, Chesapeake, and curly-coat. A fast maturity rate is not an unmixed blessing, nor is a slow maturity rate a serious problem. The slower breeds generally retain their training better, whereas the faster ones require frequent refreshers throughout their lives.

Different dogs within a breed mature at different rates. Not every Labrador races through his training the way those that have made the breed so popular do.

Some trainers train faster than others, too. I am one of the slower ones. I value style, slash, and dash so much in my dogs that I do everything I can to retain it. You can't put it back after you have destroyed it. Thus, I take more time, under-work my dogs to keep them eager, and use as many positive motivators as I can.

If you wonder how long it will take you to complete your retriever's initial training, please heed my admittedly unsatisfying answer: It takes as long as it takes. It depends on your dog. It depends on you.

Further, even after you complete his initial training, you should continue working him the rest of his active life. There are always new tests to teach him. He will always need a little work here or there. If you run him in field trials or hunting tests, you must train hard all the time to keep him really sharp. Besides, he loves to work, and you love to work him. So, what's your hurry?

More relevant schedule questions are: How often should I train my retriever? And, how long should each session last?

Training retrievers is more labor-intensive than training either pointing dogs or flushing spaniels. The retriever must be under better control. The retriever must be taught so many more things that are not natural, especially in the blind retrieve. Even the multiple mark training, which is partially natural, requires an unbelievable amount of training. Switch-proofing is a gradual process. The many terrain, cover, water, and wind conditions affect multiple marks so much more severely than they do singles. The sequence of the falls can make a test easy or difficult. The handler interacts with his retriever more often, more closely, and more continuously, than does the handler of either the pointing dog or the flushing spaniel. This is not a criticism of the latter two types of hunting dogs. I have owned several of them, including Flicker, my current Springer-in-residence. I have enjoyed working and hunting with them, and prefer them for certain types of upland work. However, their training consists more in allowing them to develop their natural abilities and less in control training. That is why I say retriever training is the most labor-intensive.

Thus, it should surprise no one that the more time you can spend training a retriever, without over-working him at any one time, the better he will become. However, most of us work for a living, so we cannot spend all our waking hours creating a retrieving wonder. Besides, most of us have family and other social obligations that limit our training time even more. So, instead of talking about optimal time commitments, let's talk about what most of us can reasonably do.

Puppy training, obedience, and force-breaking require frequent short sessions. Two or three brief periods per day are ideal. Since you do all this training at home, you should be able to approximate that amount of time.

Field work (marks and blinds) requires that you leave home. If you can have three or four evening sessions per week plus one or two each weekend, you will make excellent progress. To prevent over-working your dog, limit him to two activities per session. Two marking tests, two blind retrieve drills, or one marking test and one blind retrieve drill. If you must rerun something so often that he appears tired, put him up and continue after he rests, or even wait until tomorrow.

Those who work daytime jobs must limit their weekday training to the months of daylight saving time, April through October. Weekend training often gives way to hunting during the fall—as it should. Across the northern part of the country, snow limits training through the winter. So most amateur trainers have to make due with six or seven months of serious training per year. More would be better, but the realities of life must prevail.

Handling Techniques

Because operating a retriever is such an interactive process, you should train yourself as well as your dog. Your handling techniques must be clear and consistent if you are to communicate with the other half of the team, especially when he is some considerable distance away, as he will be when you handle him to a blind retrieve.

You must be clear and consistent in the way you set your dog up, the way you send him, the way you blow the whistle, the way you give him arm signals, even the way you take a bird from him. In every chapter, I explain the handling techniques you should use for the work involved. I admit there are alternative approaches, but what I present here is clear and consistent—and has worked for lots of folks with lots of retrievers.

You must use handling techniques in the early stages of training that make both your jobs easier. I call these techniques the KISS system (Keep It Simple, Stupid). Basically, you start every test standing up with your retriever sitting at heel. Later, after he can handle the work involved, you can introduce the more exotic handling situations that simulate actual hunting: sitting on a stool, pointing a gun at the bird; sitting in a blind with the dog outside somewhere; lying down in a grain field; walking birds up with your dog at heel; and so forth.

If you will think of your handling techniques as ways to communicate with your retriever, you will make few mistakes. You're the quarterback. He's the rest of the team. You call the plays. You give the snap count. The rest of the team keys off every sound you utter, every move you make. If you are clear and consistent, the rest of the team will do the right thing. If you are erratic and unpredictable, you will experience one broken play after another.

One evening, when I was a child back in the 1930s, I greeted my Dad at the front door by shoving a newspaper right in his face and shouting, "Look, Dad, it says in Ripley's column that pro quarter-back Sammy Baugh knows 5000 plays! Wow, Dad, 5000 plays!"

Dad grinned and answered, "Doesn't mean much if the other ten guys don't know them, too."

Your Training Group

It is extremely difficult to train a retriever alone. In marked retrieves, you can't throw far enough to challenge your dog's marking ability. Besides, it is tough to control and handle a dog while tossing two or three dummies as far as you can. You need helpers to throw for you, and you need dependable helpers, ones who will be there every time, ones that take a serious interest in what you are doing.

Throwing dummies and birds for retrievers is not the most exciting work in the world. You slog through all sorts of cover, wade or row in water, just to get in position. You wear insect repellent to prevent mosquito and chigger bites. Even so, you are often plagued by flying insects. You must throw exactly the same over and over, and stand perfectly still while the dog works, which sometimes seems like forever. You must also be willing to have all this fun several times a week through the entire training season.

Many beginners blithely dream that their non-doggy spouses will do this for them. My wife taught me the folly of such dreaming years ago. She is well-coordinated and athletic enough to jitterbug all night or until I beg for mercy (whichever comes sooner—and you can guess which does). In our younger days, when we had snowball fights with the kids, she could cream me nine times out of ten when I was running a crossing pattern. Nevertheless, when I prevailed on her to throw dummies for me with my first retriever, all her coordination deserted her. She threw them behind her, off to the wrong side, straight up in the air, anywhere but where I wanted them.

Ditto for kids. I was more fortunate there, but most people aren't. Two of my kids went through a period when they trained and trialed with me. I started another throwing so young that he never suspected that every kid on earth wasn't out tossing dummies for Dad every night. My other kids followed their mother's example.

For most retriever trainers, the only reliable long-term solution is a training group of three or four committed retriever nuts, each with no more than two dogs. Any more people or dogs-per-person makes it difficult to work every dog every session. Most of the dogs should be in the same general phase of training. Ideally, one member should be an experienced trainer who can help the others.

Where do you find such a group? First, talk to the breeder from whom you bought your pup. If he is local, he may have such a group you can join. When I was breeding my Rumrunner Goldens, I always invited local puppy buyers to join my group. It not only kept me well supplied with throwers, it also allowed me to watch the pups develop. If the breeder is not local, he may know of someone in your area who has a group you can join.

If the breeder can't help you, check out the local retriever field trial club, the local hunting test club, or the local breed club. If none of these exist in your area, advertise in the classified of your local paper or company house organ.

Training Grounds
Your backyard will suffice for most of your obedience training and force-breaking.

Every type of actual retrieving work (single marks, double marks, blind retrieves) can be started on bare ground in town—schoolyards, parks, vacant lots. In fact, the initial steps in each not only can be done on bare ground, but can best be done there, rather than in cover. You should train through trial-and-success first, then reinforce with limited trial-and-error. Success in the initial steps of each type of retrieving work depends on the dog finding the dummy every time. That happens on bare ground. It may or may not happen in cover.

However, over the life of your retriever, you will do most of your work in cover. Thus, you need suitable training grounds out in the country. Suitable grounds consist of a large land area with all the terrain and cover variations you need to train your dog to handle. That varies from locale to locale. Suitable grounds must also include adequate water. Frequently, one large lake offers less than several small ponds, especially if the ponds have cover, stick-ups, points, island, and cover in the water.

Most retriever field trial clubs and hunting test clubs have leases on grounds that members can use for training. If there is such a club in your area, join it.

However, you need more than one place to train. Dogs trained exclusively in one place frequently act as if they have never been trained when taken somewhere else.

If there is a spaniel club in your area with leased land, join it too if they will let you train retrievers on their lease. Ditto for any pointing breed club. Neither of these clubs will likely have much in the way of water, but at least you gain some additional land.

I currently belong to a duck hunting club near my home town. Naturally, it has outstanding water for retriever training, and it isn't all that expensive to belong.

I have gained access to excellent land and water by simply showing the land owner what I do with my dogs. They watch awhile, see that my dogs are under control, and tell me to come out any time—free.

Many states have public lands that are open to dog training at certain times of the year. Contact your Fish and Game Commission for locations and schedules.

However and wherever you get the training grounds you need, use common sense when you go there. Remember you are a guest, even if you are paying a steep fee to lease the place. Close the gates you open. Don't knock fences down. All the dos and don'ts of hunting and fishing apply.

I remember when one retriever field trial club in my area lost a good lease through the unbelievable stupidity of two members. It was a hot and dry summer. The pasture grass was beige and brittle. The ponds were low. At dusk on the Fourth of July, these two members brought their wives and kids out to the lease and started shooting

fireworks! Fortunately, the farmer threw them out before they ignit-
ed the entire county. Asked about it later, one of the culprits said,
"Hell, we lease the place. We ought to be able to do anything we
want out there." The farmer relieved them (and the rest of the club)
of any further opportunity to experiment on his land.

Procrastination

Put off procrastination every chance you get—and you will get lots
of chances through your retriever's active life.

You will not get many opportunities during your pup's first few
weeks at your place. He's cute. He's fun. Besides, you have to feed
him so often, water him so often, clean up after him so often, let him
in and out so often that procrastination doesn't really have a fair
chance to play.

When you start formal obedience training, the odds begin to
change. "It's raining—sort of—so I can't work him tonight." "Hey,
in 30 minutes I have to take my son to practice. I haven't got time
to work young Feather-Fiend." "Look, I worked late at the office.
My boss is an SOB that no jury would convict me for killing. And
I'm tired." "So I got up a little late. You want me to do without
breakfast just to heel this mutt around on the patio? I'll do it after
dinner, honest."

During single marked retrieve training, procrastination draws
some good cards. "It rained two days ago. No way could we get into
that pasture now." "Joe can't make it, and Harry's such a lousy
thrower I might as well not go." "He's dropping the dummy five
feet in front of me. May as well hang it up until I force-break him."

During force-breaking, procrastination has you beat with its up-
cards. "I'm just not getting anywhere. He won't hold it by himself."
"My back aches from leaning over to pick up the dowel every time
he spits it out while heeling." "Every time I hold the dowel in front
of him, he looks away." "I'm no sadist. I shouldn't have to apply
force this often."

During double marks, you start drawing some gut-cards. "He
keeps switching, but maybe he's getting the idea. Still, I'd rather watch
TV tonight." "Damn it, why can't he remember that memory bird?

Well, maybe if I give him tomorrow off." "He did it! He did it! No need to push him any farther this week."

By the time you get into blind retrieve training, you're drawing nothing but aces, and procrastination is thinking about folding. "Look at that! He's going to the cone I aimed him at." "Wow, what a cast! I could do this all day!" "Let's see. A soft OVER should suffice here. It worked! It worked!"

The more battles you win with procrastination, and the earlier you win them, the more certain that you will one day have a working retriever you can be proud of, one your friends will envy and rave about.

The real secret is to put off procrastination until you retire your retriever.

The Professional Retriever Trainer

There are two popular schools of thought about pros, and I don't agree with either of them.

On the one hand, there are those who feel totally incompetent to train retrievers. They turn the entire job over to a pro, and only see the dog during hunting season or at field trials. Their attitude is, "Hey, I don't have time to train a retriever. Yeah, I wish I knew my dog better, but look at all the trophies and titles he has. Wouldn't have them if I hadn't put him with a pro."

On the other hand, there are those who feel it would be a disgrace to get help from a pro. "I can train my own dog, thank you. Don't need any help. So what if he breaks at the sight of incoming birds, drops the ones he retrieves in the mud at the edge of the water, and eats one now and then. That's plenty good enough for a hunting dog."

In my frequently disputed and often erroneous opinion, the pro's greatest usefulness among hunters lies between those two positions. You train your dog, but when you run into a particularly baffling problem, you confer with your pro (and pay him for his services, naturally).

That is the approach I have always taken, and the one I recommend to you. No one knows everything about retrievers, so you should feel no shame if you occasionally hit a snag you can't work out. Pros go to other pros for help now and then, just as golf pros do.

Here and there during the training program I present in this book, I tell you that if your dog behaves in such-and-such a way, you should take him to a pro for an evaluation. That is good advice every time I offer it. It is advice I would follow myself.

When you go to a pro, be honest with him. It will save you money. If your dog is blinking, or bolting, or eating birds, don't save face by telling the pro, "Hey, this is a great dog, been doing everything just fine. I don't have time to finish him up right now, but you won't have any problem doing it."

That initial lie sets up the next one. The pro discovers the dog's problem, and in order to solve it as quickly as possible, he calls the owner to find out when and how it started. The owner's ego is now at stake, so he says, "Hey, what have you done to my dog? He didn't do anything like that when I brought him in. I'm not about to pay you after you messed him up like that."

Pros can deal with the dogs that come through the front gate. It's the owners that make life difficult.

If you take your dog to a pro, be honest with him. Tell him up front what the problem is, how it started, how long it has been going on, and what cures you have tried. Then, answer his questions honestly. You won't shock him, for he has heard it all many times over. He just wants to work your dog through whatever problem it has as quickly and cheaply (for you) as he can.

GO WITH GOD

Enough handshaking. Your glass is empty and your pup needs to relieve himself.

Reflect on what I have said here awhile before you read the next chapter. Spend the rest of the evening playing with the pup, and read again tomorrow after work.

However, don't try the read-a-page/train-a-page approach, nor even the read-a-chapter/train-a-chapter. Neither works. Instead, read the entire book, maybe more than once, to get a complete picture of where you are going and how you will make the trip. Only then should you go back and start studying and applying the material in Chapter Two, and so on.

You may have noticed that I have not in this first chapter discussed what it takes to be a dog trainer. There are a couple of reasons for this.

First, every time I read such a passage in a book, I get a deep feeling of insecurity. The preternatural traits so many writers prescribe just to teach a retriever to run out and pick up a bird intimidate me, even now after I have done it time after time for over 30 years.

Second, I think any healthy and rational person can train a retriever if he really wants to. You only need to know two things: the techniques in an integrated training program; and *your dog*. I give you the former in this book. Your dog tells you all about himself every moment you are with him. If you pay attention, you cannot avoid understanding him.

Granted, some people have more talent as dog trainers than others. They are more insightful, more creative, and probably much more interested than the general population. Some athletes play in the major leagues, some in the various levels of the minors, and some peak out in slow-pitch softball. Yet they are all ball-players, all athletes.

If you want to train a retriever, you can train a retriever. *Vaya con Dios.*

Puppy Training

GETTING ACQUAINTED

OK, you have a nicely bred puppy of seven to twelve weeks old. He has been checked by your veterinarian; he is properly housed and fed; and you are wondering what to do next. There are a lot of things that need to be done as soon after weaning as possible.

First off, get acquainted with the pup. Everything in your future training program depends heavily on the rapport between trainer and trainee, so start to develop that immediately. Establishing rapport does not mean pampering the pup, giving in to his every whim—nor does it mean dominating the infant animal into abject submission. No, rapport requires that you and your pup develop a deep mutual affection, that you respect each other's rights, that you understand each other's feelings, and that you share a common understanding of priorities. This demands two things from you: *consistency and insight.*

> This puppy may be retrieving only a sock, but hey, a guy's gotta start somewhere!

Consistency is the more difficult for most of us. If, for example, you decide that it is wrong for your pup to get up on the furniture, it must be wrong every time—not just when it especially disturbs you. Likewise for jumping up on you. If it is permissible when you are wearing old clothes, you can hardly expect the dog to act differently when you are dressed up. Personally, I love to have my dogs jump up on me; I pet them, talk to them, and hug them when they do. Consequently, if I am dressed up, I cannot go out in the back-yard when they are out of their runs, so I keep an old pair of cover-alls near the back door for such situations.

Figure out what your rules are going to be, how you will enforce them, and then be consistent—and make sure that everyone else in the family is consistent, too.

Insight is easier. Simply observing your pup's reaction to his environment day by day will tell you whether he is affectionate or aloof, sensitive or tough, quiet or active, submissive or dominant, and so on. There is no "ideal" set of characteristics, but every train-er will tend to favor a certain kind of dog. I, for example, most enjoy working with dogs that are affectionate, sensitive, somewhere in the middle in the submissive/dominant scale, and very active. Such a dog responds well to training, and yet exhibits the style I find pleasing. He will not withstand much harsh punishment—nor will he often need it. On the other hand, I find it difficult to relate to the aloof, tough, dominant type dog. Such a one insists on a heavy hand from the trainer, but seems to shrug it off with no ill feelings. This dog wants to be reminded who is boss frequently, and respects only the trainer who is not reluctant to remind him. Although I can work successfully with one of these hard-boiled ani-mals, I don't enjoy it.

If you find that your pup is developing a personality that you dis-like—too tough, too sensitive, too energetic, or too submissive—you should consider trading him in on a new model. You will spend a lot of your recreation time for the next few years with a retriever, so why not get one you enjoy?

As long as you allow the pup enough time to sleep—and they seem to do a lot of that at first—you cannot spend too much time getting acquainted. However, if you have to spend several hours away from home each day, you will have to wedge in your dog time around your work. A few minutes in the morning and a longer period in the evening will do nicely, especially when complemented with a gener-ous weekend allotment. During these times you will come to under-stand your pup—and, more importantly, the pup will come to under-stand you. Dogs read people better, faster, and more thoroughly than

people do dogs. Given ample exposure to you, that pup will do most of the adjusting without you even realizing it.

During this familiarization period, introduce the puppy to as many of the things he will have to cope with through his life as possible. How to go up and down stairs. The sound of the doorbell. The TV. The washing machine. The dishwasher. The trashmen. Take the pup for walks around the neighborhood and let other people make up with him. An occasional trip to a shopping center is an excellent idea.

To establish rapport with your puppy, you should spend lots of time with him. Not just training time, but also "buddying around" time, as the author does here with the Chesapeake pup, Beaver. *Photo by Theresa Spencer*

Of course, take the pup out into the field and let him experience cover and terrain variations. The earlier the young dog encounters these things—as long as the introduction is non-threatening—the better. Whenever the pup appears fearful, give him more time to get used to the object of his fear, but don't coddle him (or you will be training the dog to act fearful in order to be petted). Stay calm and let the dog work out his own problem. You just provide the opportunities.

EQUIPMENT

You need a collar for your pup. Actually, you need a series of them in graduated sizes to accommodate his increasing neck size. I prefer the little nylon strap collars with plain buckles on them. They are cheap and sturdy. Later, when you start obedience training, you will need a chain training collar, but not now.

You should have a leash, or lead (as doggy folks call them). Start out with a six-footer about 3/8" wide. These come in leather and webbing. I prefer leather, but webbing is fine, too, and cheaper.

You need a puppy-sized retrieving dummy. Again, you need a series of them in graduated sizes. My wife makes mine from pillow ticking and foam-rubber chunks. Several mail-order catalogs offer these dummies in a variety of materials. Take your choice.

If your pup resists returning to you with the dummy, you will need a 15- or 20-foot rope with a snap on one end and a loop tied in the other. Go to your local hardware store and find rope that seems

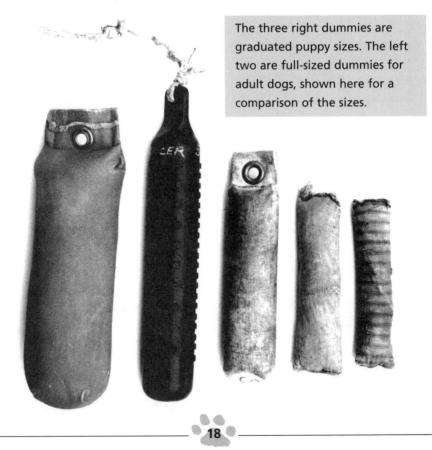

The three right dummies are graduated puppy sizes. The left two are full-sized dummies for adult dogs, shown here for a comparison of the sizes.

appropriate—neither too fine and tangly nor too heavy and cumbersome—and make your own.

If you must use a rope on your pup, you need a stout pair of leather work gloves to protect your hands from friction burns.

A series of puppy strap collars, with an adult strap collar at the bottom.

THE PUPPY'S NAME & NO

The first word you want to teach the pup is his name. Not his long-winded registered name, but a short call-name you will use daily for the rest of his life. This call-name may or may not be derived from the registered name. My Brandy was registered as Rumrunner's Brandy. Duffy was Duncan Dell's MacDuff. And so on. Others choose names with no relationship to the dogs' registered names. "Jake" might be registered as JoJo's Frightful Fantasy, or something equally unrelated to the call-name.

Two things are necessary in a call-name: It should be short, no more than two syllables; and it should not sound like any other word in the dog's vocabulary, especially the various command words you will teach him: NO, HUSH, KENNEL, RELEASE, SIT, HEEL, STAY, COME, BACK, OVER, FETCH, GIVE, DOWN.

You will use the dog's call-name to get his attention most of the time, so a short one will serve you better. "Sweet Penelope" might sound endearing as you fondle and pet the little puppy, but over the dog's entire life, you will find just plain "Penny" more comfortable.

A person should seldom shout at his dog. However, when shouting is called for—and it may save the dog's life some day—a short name "shouts" better than a long one. One or two syllables, no more.

Call-names that sound like command words—Kit (SIT), Mack (BACK), Ray (STAY), Joe (NO), and so forth—will cause your dog to misunderstand you at times, especially at a distance. Sometimes you will get some strange responses, like having the dog take off when you want to stop him. You holler MACK and he hears BACK.

Having selected a good call-name, you should start teaching the youngster to respond to it. If you are a puppy cuddler (as I am), repeat the name as you carry the puppy around the house and yard. Over and over and over. Look at it like this: You have to say something to the pup while carrying him, so why not say his call-name? That way, he can learn something from your voice. Use that name when you put the food bowl down, when you go outside to let the pup out of his run, when you run away from him in play and he is chasing you.

Later you will occasionally use the dog's call-name when you are displeased. Now, however, use it only under pleasant circumstances. If the pup comes to associate the sound of his

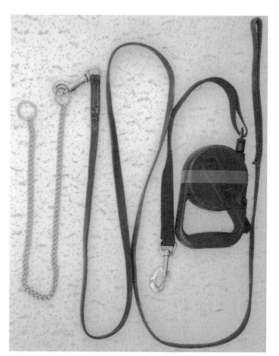

A six-foot lead with a chain training collar attached. Also a Flexi-Lead, which is handier than a rope working with a puppy that doesn't want to return with the puppy dummy.

name with rewards of various kinds—being held and petted, being fed, being let out of the run, chasing the boss around the yard, and so on—he will come to react positively to that name. If the pup associates that sound with unpleasantness, he will react negatively, and perhaps run away from you when you say his name, or at least ignore you. If the pup is sometimes rewarded and sometimes punished when he responds to his name, he will become one bewildered youngster.

Initially, the only word the pup should associate with your displeasure should be NO. A normally inquisitive pup will get into enough mischief to learn quickly that NO means trouble. Use NO, without the pup's name, whenever you correct the dog for anything.

Of course, you must back up your NO's with whatever little force is necessary to gain compliance with your wishes. Pups of seven weeks to four or five months are easy to handle physically, so little actual punishment is necessary. Simply forcing the pup to do or stop doing something normally suffices. On those occasions where more is needed, a good shake by the loose skin on the shoulders coupled with a stern bawling out will convince most youngsters. A swat on the rump with a newspaper will do wonders. However, never strike the pup in the face with your hand—NEVER. If a retriever becomes hand shy, he will avoid taking a line to a bird from the hand he fears.

HUSH

Some puppies are naturally quiet; others are naturally noisy; most fall somewhere between. Regardless, if you are a city-dweller, with neighbors to consider, you must train your dog to stop barking on command.

Personally, I like to use the short word HUSH as the command word for this. Some prefer STOP-THAT-NOISE or SHUT-IT-UP, but the simple, one-syllable HUSH works as well and is easier to articulate when you are sleepy. Whatever command you use, the trick is to get the dog to understand that it means stop barking—NOW.

Sometimes in the middle of the night, before you are able to dress and go out to correct the dog, he may stop temporarily on his own. Then, as soon as you have snuggled back under the covers, he starts up again. I have found that the dog learns what HUSH means quickly if I open a window and say HUSH firmly while the dog is still barking, and then go out and grab his muzzle and shake it while repeating HUSH several times. Even if the dog stops barking before I get outside, this seems to convey the meaning of HUSH nicely. After a few such corrections, most dogs stop barking when I open the window and command HUSH.

Another good punishment for barking is squirting water from the hose in the dog's face. Naturally, this can only be done in the summer in most areas of the country. Again, command HUSH through the window, then go out and squirt the dog while repeating HUSH several times.

Whichever punishment you use—and I use them both in season— always repeat HUSH several times as you administer it. This allows the dog to associate the discomfort with the command word. Then, later when you use the command word alone, the pup will stop barking because of that association.

You should not begin this HUSH training as soon as your new puppy arrives. Look at things from his point of view: He has been removed from his mother and littermates, perhaps flown several hundred miles in an airplane, picked up by a total stranger, driven to a strange house, played with awhile, and then placed in an unfamiliar kennel run after dark. No wonder that the poor thing howls a bit the first few nights.

Still, you must consider your neighbors. If you take the new pup around and introduce him, explaining that he may be a little noisy for a few nights, most people will be understanding. Then, if you get out of bed and reassure the pup whenever he becomes noisy in the night, he won't become totally obnoxious. The best way to handle the new pup at night is to go out whenever he bays, let him out of his run, and allow him to follow you around the yard until he is sleepy again. Then, put him up and go back to bed. Don't pick him up. Don't pet him. Don't make a fuss over him. Just keep him walking until he is ready to sleep again, which doesn't take long for a just-weaned puppy. This rather impersonal approach prevents the dog from feeling that he is training you to come out and console him. After a few nights of this, when the pup is acclimated to his new environment, you can start HUSH training.

HUSH training brings out the contrariness in some dogs. Even though they may obey the command, they find subtle ways to get even with the humanoids who interfere with their "normal" canine communications.

Katie, a Lab bitch I owned several years ago, had her own way to avenge this training. Dutifully quiet at night, she acted as my personal alarm clock on weekends, when I tried to get a little extra sleep. About fifteen minutes after my regular weekday wake-up time, she would give me a quiet little WHOOF. I ignored it. A few minutes later, she would send me another WHOOF, this time a little louder. I ignored it. The WHOOFS would get louder and more frequent until I commanded HUSH. She would be quiet for a while, but eventually she would WHOOF again. Then I went out, shook her muzzle and commanded HUSH. I also let all the other dogs out, leaving Katie in her run as punishment, and went back in the house. After waiting until she had been quiet for several minutes, which was very difficult for her with the other dogs running free, I let her out. We went through this series of chess moves every Saturday and Sunday, and I was never sure who was the trainer and who the trainee. I won every battle, but never the war.

Beaver, my current resident Chesapeake, seldom barks. However, immediately after I HUSH any of the other dogs, he gives me an indignant WHOOF, as if to say, "OK, you yelled at me for no reason, so you owe me one. Here it is." Oh, well.

PLAY-RETRIEVING

Many beginners create all manner of problems by starting play-retrieving as soon as they get the pup home. They cannot wait to experience the wonderful "retrieving instinct" they have heard about. Always a mistake, this can be a disaster if the dog is a bit soft and the owner too demanding.

The new puppy should not be asked to retrieve anything for a while. How long? Well, like everything else, it varies from pup to pup, but there are two things that should happen before you start play-retrieving with your youngster: First, he should establish his "lair;" and second, he should form a definite attachment to you, the trainer.

Every dog establishes a lair. It is that one special place he considers his own, the place to which he retreats to sleep, meditate, or just get away from the tribulations of everyday life. For the outside dog, the lair will be the dog house. For the inside dog, it will be where he sleeps. For reasons that will soon become apparent, you should delay play-retrieving until after your pup has established his lair.

Further, it is worse than pointless to try play-retrieving until the youngster feels that you are his special human, his buddy and his boss. Through early familiarization you become his buddy. Through NO and HUSH training, you become his boss.

The so-called "retrieving instinct" does not incline the dog to bring things to a person, as is commonly thought. No, it is an instinct to pick things up and tote them back to the lair. Delivery to the trainer must be taught. Initially, this training takes the form of "tricking" the dog into delivering when his intention was to run to his lair. The trainer places himself in the dog's path and cons the dog into delivering as he goes by. Later, conditioning and the dog's feelings for the trainer make him (the trainer) an artificial lair while retrieving.

To initiate this conditioning, first, familiarize him with a puppy dummy of appropriate size. Hold him by the collar, and show him the dummy. This is something new and many puppies are a bit apprehensive. Let him smell it and mouth it a bit. However, don't let him run off with it. Control the pup with the collar and keep the dummy in your hand, even while he mouths it. This initial step is simply one of familiarization. Don't try yet to get the dog excited about the dummy by teasing with it. At first, that could frighten some pups and set training back.

When you are sure the dog has no fear of the dummy, go near his lair. Release your grip on the collar and tease the pup with the dummy. Tap it on the ground in front of him; wave it in the air above his head; and so on. When he is frantic to get it, toss the dummy four or five feet. If all goes well, the pup will pounce on it, spin around, and head for his lair. Since you are in the way, he must

go directly past you. As he does, grab his collar gently and stop him. *Do not try to take the dummy now.* Just bring the pup to a stop beside you.

Pet and praise the pup for several moments, all the time letting him keep the dummy. If you try to take it, you will encourage the dog to run away from you next time. In his mind, that dummy is canine property, fairly obtained, and you have no right to it. Respect that feeling. Just praise and pet the pup and make him glad

In early play retrieving, don't take the dummy as soon as the puppy brings it to you. Instead, let him hold it while you pet and praise him awhile. If you take the dummy right away, the puppy will be more inclined to run off with it next time. *Photo by Theresa Spencer.*

he "chanced by you." After a few moments of this, see whether the dog is willing to surrender the dummy. If so, take it; if not, continue the praise and petting while allowing the pup to keep the dummy. Eventually he will let you take it.

Repeat this twice more. Don't give even the eagerest pup more than three retrieves per session.

OK, that's how it goes if the pup reacts ideally. However, there are several less-than-ideal ways that a pup can react: He may not even go after the dummy; he may go after it but not pick it up; he may go out, lie down, and begin to chew on the dummy; or he may pick it up and run off.

If the pup doesn't chase after the dummy, you may not have done the preliminaries thoroughly enough. The pup may not feel comfortable with this new thing, or you may have tossed it before he was adequately excited. Start over and see if that was the problem. It is also possible that the pup is too tired from playing with the kids or other dogs. You should confine him for an hour or so before each training session so that he will be adequately rested. It is also possible that the pup may not feel well. However, if this reaction persists over several sessions, it could indicate that the pup lacks retrieving instinct. As soon as you suspect this—which should be as soon as there is no other explanation—you should take the pup to a competent professional retriever trainer for an evaluation. Why waste a large segment of your remaining life on a dog that has no real desire to do what he was bred to do?

All the same things apply to the dog that will not pick the dummy up. If he is well rested, healthy, and has been properly introduced to the dummy, but won't pick it up through several sessions, take the pup to a pro for an evaluation.

The pup that goes out, lies down, and starts chewing on the dummy will probably turn out to be a tough, independent cuss that will require a heavy hand throughout his training. Solving the immediate problem is rather simple: Go get the dummy away from the pup; then put the lead on and start again. If the dog does the same thing again, use the lead to haul him unceremoniously back to you, *with or without the dummy.*

This youngster is not given to dropping dummies, or even letting loose of them without coercion. However, if the dummy does fall out as you yank the hooligan back, keep on dragging. If you ease up, he will learn that he can control you by dropping the dummy.

The pup that runs away ("bolts") with the dummy must also be put on the lead immediately. Both of these latter two dogs—the chewer and the bolter—tend to be aloof and little affected by praise and petting, which makes it difficult to motivate them to return through anything but force and fear. Frankly, these negative motivators will play a big role in all training of such dogs. If you are too tender-hearted to apply copious force, you should consider starting over with a new pupil. If you decide to stick with what you have, there is one positive motivator that will help you through your immediate problem: food. Generally, it is a bad idea to reward a retriever with food for doing what all good retrievers should do. However, in this case an exception is sometimes in order. Use the lead to force a proper return, and then "trade" the dummy for a piece of dog food. This encourages both the return and the release. This is a bad idea with any dog that will respond to praise and petting, but some won't.

I once had a Lab pup that avoided any physical contact. If I tried to pet her, she moved away. She eventually accepted a limited amount of it as an indication that she had done something right, but she was never strongly motivated by it. Food helped bring her to me with the dummy more than anything else. Naturally, I had to keep the lead on her a long time, until all thought of not returning had disappeared.

The anticipation of food may cause your pup to drop the dummy in front of you. Don't worry about this. It is a sign that the pup is coming around. Try eliminating the treats at this point, and if things go well, you may be able to discontinue them altogether—which you should do as soon as possible. Later, you will cure the dropping problem through force-breaking. Right now it is best to accept it as you work for a proper return.

Some people seem to find it very difficult to deal with dogs that don't want to return. Two of my daughters started out with this kind of dog—they are more common than you might suspect—and neither daughter would go to the lead until strong bad habits had been formed. If you find yourself reluctant to use the lead, you would be better off starting with a new dog. The various approaches you are apt to think of for this problem won't work: having someone chase the pup to you, while you act as the safe harbor; running away and hiding in the hope the pup will come looking for you; and so on. Only the lead will work.

If you go to the lead to get a decent return, stay with it until there is not the slightest doubt that it is no longer necessary. If you frequently try your pup without the lead, you may teach him to return when the lead is on and to run away when it is not. Then you *will* have a problem.

Continue doing these short (five to ten feet) retrieves directly in front of the pup's lair until the return is automatic—whether through habit or the lead. Then, try short retrieves elsewhere in the backyard, with the lead if you have had to use it in the initial steps. This is where the relationship between you and your youngster becomes especially important. Actually, what you have been doing till now is making yourself a second lair for the pup. He has run to his original lair so many times and wound up beside you—with pleasant results—that his feelings for his lair have been transferred to you. To assist this conditioning process when you move away from the original lair, when the pup picks up the dummy, run away, clap your hands, and call the pup excitedly. Naturally, use whatever positive motivators here that you used before: praise and petting, or food.

As your dog succeeds in returning to you, move around to different places in the yard. Keep the retrieves short, and the lead handy. If the dog shows any inclination to run the wrong way, go to the lead immediately. This is a problem that will only get worse if ignored.

Your immediate goal is to get an absolutely reliable return anywhere in the backyard off-lead. Until you have that, there is no point in leaving the backyard or lengthening the tosses. Five to ten feet is enough.

And, most important, keep the sessions short. Three retrieves are plenty. You can have another session in an hour or so, but don't make any of them too long.

THE COMMANDS FOR RETRIEVING AND RETURNING

As soon as your dog is retrieving acceptably in the backyard on these short tosses, you can facilitate his later training by using the commands you will use to send him and call him back. The dog is not yet ready to be steadied—forced to wait for your command before going out to retrieve—but you can introduce the command to retrieve as the dog breaks for these short backyard retrieves. That will simplify the steadying process later. Similarly, you can introduce the return whistle command now while the dog is returning automatically.

You can use *almost* any word as a command to retrieve—there is one exception—but the two most popular are the dog's call-name and BACK.

Those who favor the dog's call-name claim that this keeps the dog from breaking when another dog is sent to retrieve, as in honoring at field trials, hunting retriever tests, and working certificate tests. If my dog goes only on "Belle," and you send yours with "Duke," there is little chance of either breaking when the other is commanded to retrieve.

Those who favor BACK claim that the dog which comes to associate going away from the handler with BACK will be easier to train on one part of the blind retrieve. In this training, the command BACK is given in conjunction with an arm signal to send the dog out farther to find the bird. This, too, is a move away from the handler. Whether dogs are perceptive enough to make this connection may be questioned, but lots of trainers use the command BACK to send their dogs for all retrieves.

Others, seeking the best of both worlds, use the dog's call-name when sending him on marked retrieves (those the dog has seen) and BACK for sending him on blind retrieves (those the dog has not seen).

Take your choice: the dog's call-name, BACK, or both. It is more a matter of choice than logic.

However, *do not use* FETCH. That is a specialized word in

retriever training. It is used exclusively in force-breaking, and never as a command to retrieve. Save that word for force-breaking and it will serve you well.

Having picked your command word, use it as the pup runs after the dummy. It will mean nothing now, but he will come to associate it with retrieving. Then later, when you steady him, he will quickly realize that this word allows him to retrieve, not the toss of the dummy.

Similarly, blow the come-in whistle as the pup returns to you. By tradition that is a long and two short notes: TWEEEEEEET-TWEET-TWEET. If you use that now when the dog is returning automatically, it will be easier to train him to come on that signal in your formal obedience training.

As you become more and more certain that your pup will return to you with the dummy, go ahead and lengthen the tosses, but stay within "backyard" length and on bare ground (or closely clipped grass). You are establishing good retrieving habits, not striving for distance or difficulty records. Trial and success, trial and success. The pup should experience success *every time* during this initial play-retrieving. If you make things too tricky too early, your youngster will give up, perhaps quit on you. Then what will you do?

After the pup swims comfortably, that is, without beating the water, give him a few short retrieves in water. But remember to keep them few and short.

You should take the dog for romps in all kinds of cover during this period. Let him get familiar with the feel and scent of the conditions under which he will do his life's work. Let him dig for field mice, chase song birds, catch toads, and plow through every type of cover you can find. Let the pup romp up and down hills, through trees, across ditches, whatever. However, don't expect him to retrieve anywhere except on bare ground at very short distances yet. Let him come to understand the field conditions he will have to deal with in trials and hunting without any pressure to succeed at retrieving.

INTRODUCTION TO WATER

While you are introducing your puppy to cover and terrain, you should also let him learn how to swim—assuming the weather and

water are not too cold. I have often started spring and early summer litters swimming at four weeks of age. By the time they went to their new homes at seven weeks, every pup was a competent swimmer—no reluctance to enter, no beating the water with the front feet.

On the other hand, I once started a dog swimming after her third birthday. No problem. Sure, she took a little longer to smooth out her stroke and become comfortable in the water, but she went on to become an excellent water dog.

The point is that a dog can be introduced to water at almost any age, but the younger he is the more quickly he will adjust. Dogs of all ages should be introduced to water in exactly the same way, just like puppies. You shouldn't try any shortcuts with older dogs. In fact, they usually take longer, so relax and be patient.

Are there any dogs that just can't adjust to water? The answer depends on what is meant by "adjust." I have never seen a normal, healthy retriever that could not learn to swim. On the other hand, I have seen several that hated every minute of it, making it impossible for them to handle advanced water work. I have wasted months of training time on a couple of these myself. If your dog doesn't come to enjoy water quickly, he never will. Get another prospect then and you will save yourself a lot of frustration.

You should never start a dog in water by tossing a dummy there for him to retrieve. Never. No matter how he loves retrieving. You would not expect the greatest field hockey player on earth to transfer his skills to ice hockey until he became comfortable on ice skates, would you? Ditto for the retriever that is good on land, but has never learned to swim.

The ideal place in which to introduce your dog to water is something like this: a lazy, firm-bottomed stream about twenty yards across with shallows on both sides and about eight or ten yards of thigh-deep water in the middle. For very young pups, say those under twelve weeks, it should be even narrower to better accommodate their size and strength.

A stream is better than a lake because you are going to introduce your puppy to water by having him follow you in. With a stream, you can go straight across and encourage the dog to come to you. In a lake or pond, you can only go out so far; if the dog refuses to follow, you will eventually have to come back to him. In the stream, you can walk farther away, which will make the pup feel that he is going to be left behind.

The stream should be slow-moving, of course, so the pup is not washed downstream as soon as his feet lose contact with the bottom. The bottom should offer good footing, too, or the pup may become frightened. Sinking down in mud to his elbows every step will not give the dog a good feeling about water.

There should be shallows on both sides so the pup can ease his way in from either side. You will be going back and forth across the pond in this work. Later, your dog will probably come to jump into the drink with a mighty splash, but initially he will want to do things cautiously. Plenty of shallow water on both sides of the swimming water makes this possible.

Naturally, there should be some swimming water in the middle. Eight or ten yards is plenty. Four or five would be better for the very young pup. The puppy should get his feet back on the bottom quickly after swimming a few strokes.

Somewhere in your area there is such a stream. Find it and get permission from one of the land owners—it will probably wind through several farms or ranches—to use it.

Put on some old jeans and a pair of tennis shoes. *You should never wear hip boots or waders when introducing pups to water, for they prevent you from feeling the water temperature.*

Walk around in the field adjacent to the stream and let your pup follow you. When you are good and warm—the weather should be pretty hot—wade into the stream and stand in the shallows. If the stream feels uncomfortably cold, get out and keep your dog from getting in. However, if the water is OK, encourage the pup to follow you in. When he does, praise him and walk up and down in the shallows. Continue to praise him as he follows you around. You might even sit down in the water and pet the dog awhile. It is important to let him find that following you in walking water is not much different from following you on land.

Through this initial phase, be sure that the pup doesn't get in deep enough to have to swim. Let him become familiar with the feel of water first. Most dogs enjoy it on the first trip, but not all. Adjust your training to the needs of your particular pup.

Next, wade across and encourage him to follow. If your pup has shown a little reluctance earlier, you should try to find a narrow place with no deep water to begin this. That way, the dog can follow you without swimming, which is a confidence-builder for this type pup. With most, however, this is not necessary. Just wade across the eight or ten yards of swimming water and encourage the pup to follow. He may balk at first, but if you stay on the other side and keep encouraging him, the dog will eventually follow.

When the puppy gets to you, really fuss over him. Your pleasure in his accomplishment will do much to give the new swimmer a good attitude towards water. Then, wander around in the field on that side of the stream awhile before trying the water again. This will allow the dog to warm up again.

Go back and forth several times each session, and praise the pup while he is in the water as well as after he reaches you.

Don't worry if your dog beats the water with his front feet, and above all don't dream up any clever techniques for curing this "problem." The youngster will work through it in time if you give him plenty of opportunities to swim. I have heard of inexperienced (and insensitive) trainers tying weights on a pup's front end, wading along pushing down on the dog's head and shoulders, and Heaven only knows what else. The only thing such nonsense can do is make the young dog hate the water.

Once your puppy is swimming reasonably well back and forth across the stream, you can have him follow you as you wade in other places. The fact that you go into the water frequently and seem to enjoy it affects the dog's attitude, so do plenty of it. Eventually, you will be able to row a boat around and have the dog swim behind for some distance. This is good exercise for both of you. Let the dog catch up and come aboard occasionally. That motivates the "chase" and makes the boat seem like a wonderful place (which will be nice later in duck hunting).

I like to let the pup learn to swim without beating the water before tossing the first dummy in the drink for him. However, I have frequently done the opposite without serious problem. If the dog is comfortable in the water, even if he is not yet an Olympic canine swimmer, a few short water retrieves are OK. However, remember both the words "few" and "short." Don't tire the young retriever with either too many (more than three per session) or too long (over fifteen yards, say) retrieves. Sometimes a water-beater will first start swimming properly while returning with a dummy. He may beat the water all the way to the dummy, but he will level out and swim beautifully on the way back. I have seen this with several dogs.

Basic Obedience Training

WHY OBEDIENCE?

More hunting partnerships are broken up each year by out-of-control dogs than by disagreements about decoy rigging, duck calling, gun and shell selection, politics or religion. This is true of any type of hunting, not just that involving retrievers.

For example, several years ago a friend invited me to shoot quail over his new two-year-old pointer. This man, who was not the doggy type, had received the animal as a gift from an out-of-state relative, who had assured him that the dog had one season's work on quail, had an outstanding nose, and would hunt all day without tiring. The relative had neglected to mention that the dog was a confirmed "bolter," that is, a dog that runs off and hunts by and for himself instead of for the gun.

That pointer was such a bolter that we only saw him three times all day. First, of course, when we let him out of his crate that morning. He glided effortlessly for about 200 yards before striking scent. Then he "walked on eggs" for fully fifty yards—he did indeed have an outstanding nose—before flashpointing and flushing a nice covey. We were still by the car, 250 yards away, so we got no shooting. The dog chased the birds over the next hill, and we did not see him for several hours.

Our second "sighting" was about noon, when the pointer raced past us at about 150 yards. My friend hollered "Whoa!" "Come!"

"Sit!" "Drop!" and every other command he could think of, but the dog ignored him and disappeared over another hill.

Finally, when we got back to the car at sundown and cased our unfired guns, the pointer showed up and jumped merrily back into his crate. He wasn't even winded after running all day. He had flushed every covey in the country, leaving us the impossible job of walking up scattered singles without a dog.

I avoided hunting with that particular friend the rest of the year, and so did everyone else after one trip.

The following year, he called me right before quail season and told me (with tears in his voice) that his pointer had been killed by poison the night before. He said that he couldn't hunt quail anymore, that it would only remind him of his dog. He was over this by mid-season, and once again hunted with other people who had dogs.

Did one of his hunting buddies poison that dog as an act of misguided kindness? I don't really think so. However, the timing—right before quail season—has always made me wonder.

That was a pointer, a breed that can be forgiven a lot of disobedience if it handles birds properly, that is, holds them staunchly until the hunters are close enough to get some shooting. Retrievers are a different matter. They must be under tight control at all times when hunting.

In the duck blind, the retriever must sit quietly until sent to fetch up fallen birds. If he barks at incoming ducks, or runs wildly around the blind when birds try to work, the hunters will get few shots. If the dog breaks to retrieve the first duck shot, he will not see all of the falls, which could result in the loss of a strong cripple. Furthermore, a retriever must do his retrieving in a controlled manner. If he spends too much time running and playing when sent to retrieve, he may spook new birds that would like to decoy. In the duck blind, it is control, control, control.

In the uplands, where a retriever can be expected to hunt like a spaniel, he must work close and flush his birds within shotgun range. If he runs too wide, and flushes birds at a distance, the boss will get no shooting. If he chases a missed bird into the next county, he could flush a lot of other birds out of range. Even when trailing a running pheasant, the dog should respond to the whistle signal to stop, so the hunters can keep up. In the uplands, it is control, control, control.

Fortunately, those marvelous folks who developed the retriever breeds were kind enough to give us controllable dogs, dogs readily trained to obedience. If you have experience with other types of hunting dogs, you will be pleasantly surprised with your first retriever. Because of their natural trainability these breeds, especially the golden, dominate AKC obedience trials, and they are numerically strong among guide dogs for the blind.

YOUR TRAINING PROGRAM

To maintain reasonable control over your retriever, you need only teach him seven commands: SIT, RELEASE, KENNEL, HEEL, STAY, COME-IN, and DOWN. Get consistently good responses to those seven and you will be the envy of every hunter in the marshes and meadows.

Your dog will probably become a legend in your neighborhood, too. Many years ago I took one of my dogs to a neighbor's house on a Sunday afternoon. During our discussion of dogs and hunting, I mentioned some new piece of equipment, and was asked if I would go home and get it. Instinctively, I told my dog to SIT and STAY before I left. When I returned no more than three minutes later, she was still sitting there, so I released her and tried to resume the conversation. To my surprise, my neighbors raved about this simple act of obedience. Later they spread the story around town. For several years I heard it over and over from different people, and naturally the story grew in the telling. It was eventually reported that she sat without moving a whisker for several hours, that she refused various treats, that a cat walked right past her, that another dog came and growled at her, and I forget what else. She became a legend, and all she had done was obey a very simple command for a very short time under ideal circumstances. Most people have never seen that sort of thing.

SIT, RELEASE, KENNEL, HEEL, STAY, COME-IN and DOWN. Seven basic obedience commands that separate a legend from an outlaw.

You can start teaching SIT and RELEASE as soon as the pup

knows his name and NO. When he understands SIT and RELEASE, you can introduce KENNEL. For HEEL, STAY, COME-IN and DOWN, you should wait until the pup is five or six months old. These commands demand more seriousness and a longer attention span than the typical puppy under that age possesses.

What about the older untrained dog? No problem really. He is already mature enough for all seven commands (each in its proper sequence). Such a dog may show a little more independence, require more physical strength from the trainer, and need more drill on some of the commands before becoming reliable. On the other hand, he is more mature, has a longer attention span, and will tolerate firmness better when he needs it.

Obedience training cannot be successfully done on a "now and then" schedule. Ideally, the dog should be trained twice a day for ten or fifteen minutes each time. Many working people cannot manage two sessions per day, so they have to make do with one. That's OK, too. However, if you are in that situation, don't lengthen your one daily session to compensate. Stick to ten or fifteen minutes.

You should train when the dog is fresh, not after field work or a play period. Confine him in a kennel run or crate for about two hours before each session. That way, when you come to give him his obedience training, he will be jumping out of his skin to get out and work with you. Training becomes a reward, something he looks forward to. He will prance through his drills.

How long should it take to complete the course in basic obedience? Well, in one sense, it is never completed. You will give your dog an occasional refresher throughout his active life to keep his responses sharp and immediate. However, the initial training doesn't take a lifetime. An experienced trainer doing two-a-days with a smart five-month-old pup could probably complete the course in five weeks. A green trainer giving one-a-days to a slow dog might take 15 weeks. Most teams fall somewhere between those extremes. However, since basic obedience training can (and should) be done in parallel with puppy field training, it really doesn't matter whether it takes five weeks or fifteen weeks. It isn't holding anything up.

TONE OF VOICE

You have probably already been exposed to the controversy over the "proper" tone of voice. Books disagree. Amateur trainers disagree. Even professional trainers disagree. Each tends to become rather dogmatic in explaining his way of speaking to a dog.

Some advocate barking commands out like a Marine Drill Instructor. They argue that this gives you the "tone of command" that will make any living thing obey. If it works for sending troops into battle, how can it fail to elicit obedience from a dog?

Others insist on soft, sweet inflections. They use Teddy Roosevelt's expression about soft voices and big sticks as justification. They also cite the positive influence such tones have on the dog.

Who's right? In my opinion, both of them and neither of them. Let me explain.

I remember my high school principal. He was quite elderly, small, thin, and very soft-spoken. Yet, he could walk into a room full of boisterous teenagers, and within seconds, the room would be totally silent except for his voice. Every kid there would strain to hear what the principal was saying. Why? Because we all knew he meant business.

I also remember a baseball coach from my high school days. He was big, strong, and emotional—booming voice, wild gestures, taut facial muscles. Did we listen to him like we did to the principal? Naw. We knew he was only bluffing. We delighted in upsetting him just to listen to him bellow.

You can't fool kids with your voice. You can't fool dogs either. *To succeed as a dog trainer, you must first convince yourself that you mean every command.* With that attitude, you can use any tone of voice you find comfortable. Without it, none will work.

To develop that attitude, study this chapter all the way through before starting your training program. You will learn techniques for communicating your wishes to your dog, techniques for motivating your dog to obey, techniques for winning trainer/trainee disagreements. That knowledge will give you a rational basis for the confidence without which you cannot succeed.

Only two things matter about your tone of voice: clarity and consistency. Clarity, for if he can't hear, he can't obey. Consistency, for a dog only understands sounds, not words. If you vary your tone, your dog will not understand you. Whatever tone you use, use it consistently. That argues strongly for going with what comes naturally rather than struggling to shout or plead.

EQUIPMENT

Collars: You need two types of collars. One is the strap collar, which comes in leather or webbing. The other is the chain training collar, sometimes erroneously called a "choke collar."

Until you start teaching your pup to heel, you can get by nicely with only the basic strap collar. I prefer webbing to leather because it stands up to repeated wetting and drying, which any retriever's collar gets.

Webbing strap collars cost little and come in many colors, with sizes from the smallest puppy 8-incher to those for breeds much larger than any of the retrievers. I keep a collar on the pup constantly, changing to larger sizes as he grows. When he is full-grown, I buy him a full-sized model with a brass nameplate carrying my name, address, and phone number, but *not* the dog's name. I'm not going to furnish a dog thief with any usable information.

The strap collar is all you need for field work, and for much of the obedience training. However, when you teach your retriever to heel, you need a chain training collar. Properly used, it will allow you to send messages down the lead to him, messages he will receive and heed, but it will not cause him serious discomfort. This collar should be large enough to slip comfortably over the dog's head, and small enough to stay on his neck when he is running loose. As you put it on, it should be slightly snug as it goes over the dog's ears. Not tight, just snug.

One word of caution before covering how to put the collar on: *Do not allow your dog to wear a chain training collar when you are not with him.* He could catch it on something and hang himself.

Although a high percentage of retriever owners apparently don't realize it, there is a right way and a wrong way to install the chain training collar, just as there is a right way and a wrong way to put on your shoes.

The chain training collar must be properly installed before the trainer can give the intended rapid-fire jerk-and-release corrections to the dog while training him to heel. Put on correctly, the collar tightens quickly and releases quickly. The dog gets the message. Backwards, the collar just will not tighten up when you want it to, and it won't release quickly enough either. The dog gets the message at the wrong time, and training is impeded.

Obedience trialers, who train the sharpest heeling dogs on earth, have perfected this jerk-and-release technique to the level of an art form. You never see the collar placed improperly on one of their dogs.

To install the collar correctly, drop the chain through one ring and hold the resulting loop in front of you with the ring that attaches to the lead at the bottom on your left. If you slide the other ring up the chain a bit, you form the letter "P." If you hold it with the lead-ring at the bottom on the right, it will form a "Q," which indi-

Left: The chain training collar in the "P" configuration, which is proper for the dog that heels on the left. If the dog is sitting on your left, put your collar in this "P," then bend down and turn slightly to put it over his head.

Right: The chain training collar in the "Q" configuration, which is incorrect for the dog heeling on the left, but correct for the dog heeling on the right.

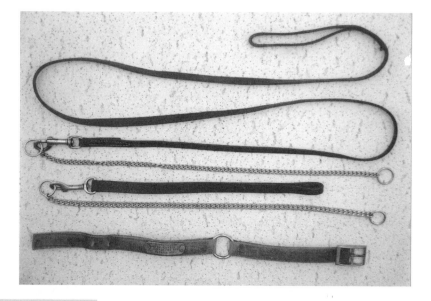

From top: A six-foot lead with a chain training collar attached; a short "traffic lead" with a chain training collar attached; a strap collar.

cates it is backwards. Form the "P" and slip the collar on the dog, and everything is right, assuming he will heel on your left, as I strongly recommend. If you insist on heeling him on the right, then the "Q" configuration is correct.

Leads: You need a basic six-foot lead in either leather or webbing. This is a handy all-around length, and the one preferred for teaching the dog to heel. I like leather because it has a better feel, and because it has enough substance to carry the messages I send quickly to the dog's collar. For average-sized retrievers, I use a lead 3/8" or 1/2" wide. For larger dogs, I go to 5/8".

Eventually, you will also buy a short "traffic" lead of 12 to 24 inches of either leather or webbing. These are very handy for hunting, trialing, getting to and from the vet's office, and so on. However, such short leads are inadequate for training a dog to heel because they don't give him enough freedom to make the necessary mistakes.

Whistles and lanyards: You need two plastic whistles on a lanyard. Why two? You will come to depend on your whistle to communicate with your retriever when he is at a distance, and you will not want any unpleasant surprises, like a broken whistle, destroying your lines of communications at a critical time.

Darrell Kincaid, a well-respected retriever field trial judge, enjoys telling the story of one of the first field trials he ever competed in. He had a pretty good young Lab entered in the Qualifying Stake, but Darrell only had one whistle on the lanyard around his neck. In the very first series, the side blew out of Darrell's only whistle, forcing him to whistle through his teeth. It didn't work too well, so his dog failed the test. As he heeled the dog off the line, one of the judges said, "Nice dog. If you ever get to where you can afford two whistles, he will do quite well in trials."

Why plastic whistles? Have you ever had your lips or tongue stuck on metal in cold weather? Plastic doesn't do that.

There are several whistles on the market, and new ones come out

Three types of lanyards and a variety of whistles. Starting from the top is a simple cord lanyard with Roy Gonia whistles; macrame lanyard with Roy Gonia whistles; braided leather lanyard with Roy Gonia whistles. Across the bottom are other types of whistles: from left, two Fox #40s, two medium Acme Thunderers, a large Acme whistle, and a small Acme Whistle.

often. Over the past several decades, the two most popular have been (and still are) the Acme Thunderer and the Roy Gonia. Some pros and some amateurs use the Acme Thunderer. Other pros and other amateurs use the Gonia. A few folks in each group get very emotional about their whistle of choice, insisting that it alone can be trusted to handle a distant retriever. My own observations indicate that the dogs don't care. They will respond to any whistle they have been trained on. Suit yourself. Use either whistle, or any of the endless stream of new-and-improved models.

You need a lanyard to keep your whistles clean and handy. There are many kinds: cheap nylon cords, single-strand leathers, expensive braided leather affairs, and colorful macrame-and-bead lanyards. Regardless of your choice, you will eventually own several. I have one hanging by the back door, another hanging from the mirror in each car, one in my duffel bag of duck hunting gear, one in my drawer full of dog training stuff, one on the peg board with my day-to-day training equipment, and two retired lanyards hanging on my den wall with the memorabilia for two favorite dogs that are no longer with me. Retriever trainers are never far from a lanyard with two whistles.

SIT, RELEASE, & KENNEL

Dog training is full of seeming contradictions. For example, the very basis of all obedience training is freedom! The dog must understand when he *is not* on command before he can become reliable when he *is* on command. Without that understanding, he will take frequent liberties just to determine his current status.

Thus, you need a specific release "command" to free the dog from control. For too many years I have used "OK"—a singularly poor choice because it is an expression used too often in ordinary conversation. I have never accidentally released a dog this way, but it is always a risk. If you have not already selected your own release command, I recommend you choose one that is not part of your day-to-day vocabulary: FREE, SCHOOL'S OUT, HAPPY TIME, or something like that. Here I will use RELEASE, which would not be a bad choice for you either.

The release command has another important role in your training program: *It allows you to praise and pet your dog for good work with no danger that he might misinterpret that as release.* Praise and petting can be powerful motivators in training a dog. However, if you allow your retriever to be released by them, you will limit yourself to punishment as a training tool, and surely you don't want that. Too frequently one hears such statements as "You can't pet a hunting dog and maintain control." That really only means that the speaker doesn't use a formal release command.

Since RELEASE is so basic to all control training, it would be nice if you could teach it first. You can't, obviously, for until you teach some other command, you have nothing from which to release him. However, you can do the next best thing: You can teach it second, right after SIT.

To teach SIT, put the collar and six-foot lead on your dog. If he is a small puppy, use the strap collar. If he is older and difficult to control physically, use the chain training collar. Either way, he should be accustomed to the collar and lead before you start. That means he should be comfortable wearing his collar and over his natural tendency to chew on the lead (one of the many NOs in a small puppy's life.)

With the collar on and lead attached, get your pup's attention and command SIT. Of course, he has no idea what that means, so you must force him into compliance by pulling up on the lead and pushing his fanny to the ground.

He is now sitting, even though he had nothing to do with it. While you continue to hold the lead taut, praise him lavishly. If he tries to move—which he will—say NO! SIT! and push his fanny down again. Then, praise him again. You are already teaching him that praise doesn't mean release. Keep him sitting a few seconds, correcting every move and praising whenever he is sitting correctly. Repeat SIT often, too.

Now, say RELEASE and force him out of the sitting position. Play with him awhile. Then, repeat the sequence again: Command SIT, force him into position, praise, correct every movement, command RELEASE, force him out of position, and play again. If possible, do this about half a dozen times per session, perhaps three or four times a day. He will quickly learn what SIT means, what RELEASE means, and he will at least suspect that praise doesn't turn him loose.

Don't try this off-lead yet, no matter how well he obeys. Later on, in your blind retrieve training, you will need an immediate response to your SIT whistle signal when your retriever is high-balling the other way at some distance. If you insist on a quick sit every time now, maintaining it later will be easier. If you remove the lead too soon, your pup will potter a few seconds before sitting—and you will learn to accept that—thereby forming a bad habit for each of you. Keep him on lead and insist that his posterior must hit the ground immediately every time you command SIT.

Next, teach him KENNEL, which means to go into his run, his crate, his dog house, or even a boat. It introduces a type of control that makes the dog easy to live with, easy to hunt with, and easy to travel with. It requires only minimal control, for it involves just one simple act: Move into the place you indicate.

If you have a kennel run for your dog, use it to teach KENNEL. If not, use a crate—one with a wire door, so your dog can see you when he is inside. That is important, as you will see.

Put the collar and lead on your dog. Now, open the gate to the run (or crate) and command KENNEL. Here again, as in the initial SIT, your dog has no idea what you want, so you must guide him with the lead. As soon as he is in the run, close the gate. Now stand there and praise him. This extends the notion that praise doesn't mean release, for the gate blocks your dog's exit from the run.

After a few moments, open the gate, say RELEASE, and encourage the dog to come out. Play, romp around, anything to make sure the pup feels no restraint.

Repeat this process five or six times during each session. Command KENNEL, pull the dog in with the lead, shut the gate, praise awhile; then command RELEASE as you open the gate; play again to make sure the pup feels complete release. Before long, the dog will go in voluntarily when you command KENNEL. The praise you give him when he is inside encourages this response. Once the youngster shows that he understands KENNEL, you can use a light form of punishment for refusals and slow responses. Jerk the lead a

Top: The author says KENNEL and the young Golden, Deuce (KC's Calidus Canis Callidus, which is Latin for "clever hot dog"), starts into his kennel run.

Middle: After Deuce is in his kennel run, the author says NO to keep him from coming out without permission.

Bottom: When given the RELEASE command, Deuce comes charging out of his kennel run. In some ways the RELEASE command is the most important obedience command . . . because it allows you to praise your dog without releasing him. This facilitates positive training throughout the dog's life.

little as you guide him in. Whenever you punish like this, be sure to praise the dog once he is in the run. The pup should come to associate praise with compliance, even when forced.

After the dog understands KENNEL and obeys it readily, you can start extending the meaning of RELEASE. Till now, the dog has come out when the gate was opened, and he probably thinks that the gate gives this freedom rather than RELEASE. Now you can teach him differently.

Command KENNEL and praise your dog in the usual manner. Then, open the gate just slightly, but do not say RELEASE. The dog will try to come bouncing out, of course. Shut the gate in his face, commanding NO rather sharply. Then, be lavish with praise—this first time can be a bit of a shock to a sensitive youngster. Open the gate again and immediately command RELEASE. If your dog is reluctant to come out, encourage him or pull him out if necessary— and then have a good play session when he does.

Repeat this several times. When you open the gate and the youngster hesitates until he hears RELEASE, you are making your point. Gradually, you can delay the time-lapse between opening the gate and saying RELEASE. Naturally, until you are certain he will stay inside, you should not open the gate too wide. If he does escape, run him down, put him back in the run, and start over.

The only verbal correction you should give the dog when he tries to escape is a sharp NO. It is not necessary to repeat the command KENNEL. You will become a better trainer if you minimize the number of duplicate commands you give. Command once, force compliance if necessary, then praise to reinforce the dog's response.

Above all, do not command STAY when shutting the gate in the dog's face. You will later teach STAY as a very strict "Don't move" or "Freeze" command. On KENNEL, you necessarily allow the pup to move around within the run. If you command STAY instead of NO when you prevent your dog from escaping, you set yourself up for some serious training problems later on when you try to teach the more rigid meaning of STAY.

Once your pup understands RELEASE, you should extend it to his everyday life. He should come to know that RELEASE frees him every time, not just when he is sitting or in the kennel run. When you take the youngster for romps in the country, always turn him loose with RELEASE. If you have to confine the dog to a particular room or area in the house when guests are visiting, let him out of that room afterwards with RELEASE. When you take him for a walk on lead, remove the lead with RELEASE once you're back home. And so on.

You should also extend KENNEL. Use it not only to get the dog to enter his run, but also a crate, a dog trailer, a car, and a boat (if you plan to hunt from a boat). Once the dog understands KENNEL for the dog run, he will pick up the expanded meaning of the command easily.

Most important of all, you should extend SIT so he will do it when you blow a single sharp blast on your whistle. Called "stopping on the whistle" and "sitting on the whistle," this is the most important command in blind retrieve training, for "if you can't stop 'em, you can't handle 'em."

Blow the whistle, immediately command SIT, enforce compliance if necessary, then praise. After a few times, your young retriever will understand that you want him to sit on either the voice or whistle command. The rest of SIT training for blind retrieves is covered in Chapter Seven. You should read that chapter and start immediately to extend SIT-on-the-whistle. Since this is the most important part of the blind retrieve, SIT training starts with a small puppy and ends only when the dog, sadly, finishes his field career.

HEEL

The dog that heels walks quietly beside the handler, typically on the left side. When the handler stops, the dog sits. This is a convenient skill for any civilized canine, regardless of breed. Especially for retrievers.

Years ago, during a season when Redheads were illegal in my flyway, I might have been arrested if my golden, Duffy, had not been trained to heel. My buddies and I had had a fair day's duck hunt, which means we had some birds but had not limited out, so we were in the blind till sundown. As we left, each hunter loaded down with impedimenta, I let Duffy run loose, knowing that he would follow me back to the car. I had not gone far when I felt Duffy nudging my leg. I stopped and he handed me a duck he had found somewhere. I switched the flashlight on and saw that it was an illegal Redhead. No one in our party had shot it. We hadn't even seen a Redhead all day. I took it and sent him on. Then, I dropped the bird and continued struggling along with my load. Fifty yards farther along, Duffy nudged me—with the same Redhead! He and I repeated this routine two or three more times before it occurred to me that we must be getting close to the car, and that there could be a game warden waiting there to check our bag. I took the Redhead from Duffy one last time, commanded him to sit, threw the illegal bird as far as I could into the darkness, and then heeled Duffy to the car. I couldn't see him, but I knew he was beside me, probably wondering what I had against that perfectly good duck. As it turned out, no game warden awaited us—the story would have been much better if one had—but you see the point.

Heeling a retriever to and from the blind becomes more and more necessary as the number of hunters using dogs on public lakes increases. Further, some hunters heel their retrievers in the uplands rather than allow them to hunt and flush before the gun. Of course, all formal retriever field activities—field trials, hunting tests, and the various working certificate tests—require heeling. Thus, if you own a retriever, you should plan on training him to heel.

I prefer waiting until the dog is at least five months old to start this, and if the dog is at all soft, six or seven months might be better.

I tried old Duffy when he was four months, and the process—gentle as it is—terrorized him. I said HEEL, stepped off, and gave the lead a little jerk. Duffy flattened out on his belly and looked at me with wildly frightened eyes. He was a hard-going, stylish dog, but he was quite soft, and something about this intimidated him. Day after day I tried. No luck. I waited until he was five months old. Again no luck. Even worse, a pattern was being established. Duffy was being conditioned to drop on his belly every time he heard me say HEEL. I waited many months, just to let him forget this pattern. When he was fourteen months old, I had my wife start him out in heeling again. The change worked. He went merrily along beside her, even forged ahead and became a little tough to control. Great!

When he was good and cocksure of himself, I took over. He was too strong for my wife to handle anyway. After that, we had no more trouble and he learned to heel very quickly.

On the other hand, Katie, a Lab female, would have been a real handful had I waited until she was past one year. She was strong, tough, and insensitive, so I started heeling her at about four months. I jerked her around until I was almost ashamed of myself, and even so barely got her attention. Each dog is a little different.

Most trainers teach their dogs to heel on their left while a few prefer the right side. I have heard it explained that the dog should heel on the side opposite that from which the person fires his shotgun. Personally, I think this is a meaningless rationalization. What possible advantage could there be for either dog or handler? Shooting is a two-handed business, so the handler doesn't have either hand free to handle the dog while shooting. Nor does the dog get any better look at the falls. Even while walking, there is no advantage in having the dog opposite the gun. We all change the way we carry our guns frequently during the day's hunt, and none of these positions would endanger a dog on either side.

Frankly, unless you have some deep emotional need to heel your dog on your right side, you would be well-advised to choose your left, which is the more popular by at least ten to one among retrieverites. All of the instructions and the photos in this book assume that the dog heels on the left, but if you opt for the right, the adjustment should be easy to make.

Your goal is to train your dog so well that he heels reliably off-lead. That way you can carry decoys, guns and shells, plus all the other gear duck hunters tote to and from the blind, and still control your dog. The slowest possible way to train a dog to this point—absolutely the slowest—is to try off-lead work frequently before your dog is ready. Like all control training, this is a conditioning process, not a learning experience as we use the term in human education. The dog is conditioned to perform properly on-lead until it becomes second nature. Even then he will need periodic refreshers when his off-lead responses become sloppy—which they will from time to time.

You condition your dog by rote drill. However, to do this

successfully, you must adopt the attitude that you are teaching your dog to take full responsibility for knowing where you are and for sticking by your side continuously. That attitude will prevent you from making the most common beginners' mistake, namely "steering" the dog with the lead.

If you keep the lead tight and steer the dog through his heeling drills, he will never be properly conditioned. Such a dog learns to follow the direction of the pressure on his neck. In human terms, you are remaining responsible for your dog's position and direction. That isn't what you want. The dog should be trained to pay attention to you and stick to your left side. That kind of training can only be done if the dog feels no pressure on his neck except when he is being corrected. Your dog should be on a loose lead whenever he is heeling correctly, and he should be corrected quickly and as sharply as is appropriate for his particular temperament whenever he strays—*whenever he strays*. That way, he will learn to pay attention to your movements and to keep near your left side, where no corrections occur.

Let's discuss the nature of these corrections, for they are critical to success. The chain training collar is one of the simplest but cleverest pieces of dog training equipment ever invented. Properly installed, it will tighten up *immediately* when the lead is jerked, and it will release *immediately* when the lead is released again. If it is tightened and loosened in a series of sharp jerks, it will quickly induce the dog to alter his direction or speed to that desired by the trainer. The dog is not dragged into position with these corrections. He is "induced," that is, redirected by a quick succession of tugs to move "voluntarily" in a new direction or at a different speed. These jerks must be somewhat unpleasant. Just how unpleasant depends on the dog. Duffy was cowed by mild little tugs, while Katie was unaffected by anything short of a hard yank.

OK, each correction consists of a series of short, appropriately

You should heel your dog on a loose lead, as Marilyn Corbin does here with her Golden, Summer (Benden's Up With The Sun). If you steer your dog with a tight lead, he will never "take responsibility" for maintaining his proper position near you.

sharp jerk-and-release tugs on the lead, which transmits the message *immediately* to the dog through the properly installed chain training collar. If the collar is improperly installed, the message will be poorly timed. It won't arrive immediately, and it won't go away right away either—which is confusing to the dog.

As soon as the dog returns to the proper heeling position, the tugs stop and the lead goes slack. The collar is always loose when the pooch is where he belongs, and it always jerks uncomfortably when he strays. That is what conditions him to pay attention and stay where he belongs. If a dog is steered with a tight lead, he will not discover the "joy" of avoiding those sharp tugs.

If the jerk-and-release technique were used alone, this training would be a negative process, and the dog would come to heel in an unsightly hang-dog manner. A lot of retrievers are so trained—and it shows!

You are more fortunate than most, however, because your dog already understands that praise does not mean release. You can praise your dog when he is doing things correctly without losing control. If you do that when your young charge is heeling correctly—and especially right after every correction—he will not only learn what you want more quickly, but he will also be a much happier working dog.

Now, some good news. There are only six mistakes a dog can make when heeling: lagging, forging, swinging wide, crowding, jumping up, and lying down. Each calls for a slight variation on the basic jerk-and-release-plus-praise technique:

LAGGING: The dog is uncertain. Give fairly gentle tugs and talk encouragingly as you do. When the dog catches up to you, praise lavishly. Don't make the mistake of slowing down or stopping for this dog. If you do, you will soon find out that he is training you.

FORGING: This is probably a bold, aggressive dog. Let the beast get ahead of you, then turn and go in the opposite direction. When this dog hits the end of the lead, give him a series of heavy jerks. Don't slow down. In fact, you might go a little faster after you turn with this character.

SWINGING WIDE: The dog is expressing independence. Turn

90 degrees away from him and, when he hits the end of the lead, give a series of moderate jerks. If the dog tends to be hard-headed, you might speed up as you turn and jerk a little harder.

CROWDING: Frequently, the dog that crowds is sensitive and feels safer when touching you. Normally, no jerks are necessary. Just turn into the dog frequently, bumping him away as you do. If the dog is not too sensitive, give him a series of fairly light jerks away from you—nothing too rough here, since the dog is trying to do things properly but is just being too cautious.

JUMPING UP: Either the dog doesn't know that this is training, not playtime, or he is trying to con you into forgetting about training. Either way, give a series of sharp jerks down, say "NO! HEEL!" and keep on walking. Praise this dog calmly. Excited praise may incite another demonstration of playfulness.

LYING DOWN: This is a real problem, one I didn't handle very well with Duffy. The dog is either frightened or trying a new method of training you. It is hard to tell which. If you are sure it is the latter, force the issue: Start walking, command HEEL, and jerk the dog along. If you are right, he will get up and play by your rules. If not, he will freeze on his belly. Stop then—don't drag him. If the dog is really frightened, find out why. Then, either help the dog over the fear or avoid the situation that brings out this response. Once I was training a dog in our unfinished basement. She heeled nicely except when I tried to go between the furnace and the sump pump. She would flatten out on her belly as soon as she realized I intended to go there. I have no idea what the problem was, but that area terrified her. After several attempts to get her over it, I decided it wasn't worth the effort, so thereafter I avoided that place in all training. We got along fine after that.

One frustrating problem that many retrievers develop after they have learned to heel is that of forging ahead while going to the line at a field trial, hunting test, or working certificate test. Once an eager retriever figures out all the excitement starts only after he gets to that special place where there are several people (judges, marshal, etc.), it becomes difficult to keep him at heel on the way.

Duffy did this so badly for a while that I occasionally had to stop him with the whistle to keep up with him. I cured him by heeling him a long ways to the line *on lead* in every training session, correcting him vigorously when he forged ahead. Lots of dogs start this annoying habit, but it only remains a problem for a trainer who will not put the dog back on lead.

OK, you now know how to correct your dog for any heeling error he can make. However, your timing is probably pretty bad. This is as new to you as it is to your dog, except that you understand what you are trying to do and he doesn't. A new trainer and an untrained dog can get all tangled up and have unbelievable problems until the trainer gains a minimal level of competence. There is a way to avoid this poor start: Don't bring the dog into the picture until you are comfortable with your part of the routine; use a friend, spouse, or offspring instead. Have this person put the lead on his right wrist and move along beside you like the dog should. I have "played dog" for a number of beginning trainers.

You can also practice your footwork while "heeling" your human

The beginner can more easily learn how to heel a dog by "heeling" an experienced trainer. The "heel-ee" can simulate the mistakes a real dog makes and help the "heel-er" make the proper corrections. Here Mary Jo Gallagher prepares to "heel" her husband Mike.

When you command HEEL, step off your with your left foot. Such consistent footwork not only reinforces the HEEL command, but also clearly separates it from STAY (when you step off with your right foot). Here Mary Jo Gallagher commands HEEL, steps off with her left foot, and her Flat-Coat, Fortune, (CH. Windfall's Flatland Fortune SH WCX), begins to walk alongside of her.

assistant around. The way you walk can help or confuse your dog. Let me explain: Your dog will come to key off of your left leg. If you move that left leg consistently while heeling, it will help your dog maintain his proper position. If you are sloppy and inconsistent, your dog must guess what you are going to do next much of the time.

For example, if you always step off with your left foot when you start heeling, your dog will be able to respond more quickly to your command HEEL. Your left leg is more visible to him. More than that, if you always step off with your right foot when leaving your dog on a STAY command, there will be a clear distinction between your actions on HEEL and STAY, and your dog will easily pick up the difference.

People who regularly compete in obedience trials are very consistent in their footwork. Their dogs must heel with absolute accuracy, so they give them all the assistance possible. They have specific foot patterns for starting, stopping, turning right, turning left, and turning around, all done with a smoothness that makes it difficult for the untrained observer to notice.

This level of perfection is not necessary for a field retriever, nor is it even possible to be completely consistent in your footwork under hunting or field trial conditions. However, you should form good habits now. Here are the foot patterns I recommend:

1. When starting to move from a stopped position, always step off with your left foot as you command HEEL.

2. When stopping, always move your left foot up to your right as the last step. Also, don't stop abruptly; slow down gradually. The stop will not surprise your dog this way.

3. Later, when teaching STAY, always step off with your right foot as you command STAY.

4. Do not make your left and right turns too sharp. Round them as much as possible to make it easier for your dog to follow you.

5. When reversing directions, always turn away from the dog; don't turn into him.

Now, practice these basic foot patterns while heeling your human assistant around the yard. Have your surrogate canine simulate the six heeling mistakes described above, so that you can practice the proper corrections. Have him forge, lag, swing wide, crowd, jump up (by raising the arm with the collar on it), and pull down like a dog lying down. Make the proper correction for each movement, and do it until it becomes instinctive, which may take a few sessions. Practice those sharp little jerk-and-release corrections, and practice the immediate praise, too. However, if any non-doggy person sees this seemingly insane process, you may end your training session running from someone with a butterfly net.

When you feel yourself ready to train your dog, put the collar and lead on, toot your whistle sharply to get the animal to sit, then command HEEL and step off at a moderate pace. The dog won't have any idea what HEEL means, of course, but you will quickly teach him that he can avoid a lot of uncomfortable jerks on the neck by walking along at your side. It is unfortunate that you can't sit down and explain—as you could to a child—exactly what you want. You must communicate through the lead and collar, and that has some negative overtones. You can minimize the negative and maximize the positive by giving the poor animal as much praise as possible as often as possible. Remember: Initially, at least, the dog is not being obstinate; he just doesn't know what you want yet.

Stop frequently, and toot the SIT whistle each time you do. This does two things: It gives the dog a command he understands in the midst of all this confusion; and starts the "automatic" sit, which he should do each time you stop while heeling.

It won't take the average retriever long to figure out what you want. Then, vary your speed—normal, slow, normal, fast (run a bit)—just to convince him that he must always adapt to your speed. No sudden bursts, no sharp reductions of speed. Just the kind of changes of pace that could occur in a day's shoot.

After your dog heels nicely in the backyard, try introducing distractions. Have family members come out and talk to you and to the dog, but insist on good heeling—all on lead, of course. When your retriever has adjusted to that, have someone bring a cat into the yard, and force the dog to heel in spite of the distraction. If possible, have other people heel other dogs around while you heel your dog, too.

Finally, take your dog to a shopping center. There are so many distractions in shopping centers that they make ideal final proving grounds for many obedience commands. You do have certain responsibilities, however, like being sure that there are no other dogs that are not under control, and that well-meaning passers-by do not interfere with your dog's response to your commands. You are there to train your dog, not to collect a lot of "oooh's" and "aaah's." Above all, don't give in to the temptation to tighten up on the lead and guide the dog around so that he looks good in front of all these strangers. Loose lead, jerk-and-release corrections, and plenty of praise, just like in the backyard.

Heel him to and from the line during his field training, but keep him on-lead for months. Even after you are confident that he will heel OK off-lead, only try it now and then. Use the lead most of the time in field training all his life. That keeps him sharp when heeling off-lead while hunting or running in trials or tests.

STAY

STAY means "Do not move," "Freeze." You shouldn't use it to bring your dog under control, but only to lengthen the period of control. You should teach your dog to STAY in a sitting position first, then in a lying position, and perhaps later while standing. For most hunting situations, this last is not necessary.

The command STAY has many uses. First, you need it when you teach your dog to take hand signals from a distance in blind retrieve training. You position your dog, command STAY, walk some distance away, turn and give the appropriate hand signal. You must do this over and over, so if your dog won't stay put, blind retrieve training sputters and stalls.

In duck hunting you occasionally must position your dog some distance from the blind. If he doesn't understand STAY, the quality of your hunting deteriorates—as well as your relationships with your hunting partners.

Around home, STAY has an important place. For example, when guests arrive, you should be able to delay an enthusiastic canine greeting until everyone is seated. Earlier I related how one of my dogs impressed the neighbors by STAYing in their living room while I ran home.

However, STAY is not a magic potion for all canine behavior problems. Most especially, it should not be used in an attempt to bring an unruly beast under control. If, for example, your dog is about to jump up on you, do not command STAY. Say NO, SIT. If your dog is about to exit from his kennel or crate when you don't want him to, command NO! You should reserve STAY for those occasions when you need to keep the immobilized dog in his current position for a period of time.

Start teaching STAY as soon as your dog shows signs of understanding HEEL, surely within a week or so of starting HEEL.

You can teach STAY easily, if you don't get in a hurry. You only ask the dog to sit there and do nothing, which is no great accomplishment, really. Most retrievers learn this quickly, and thereby mislead the inexperienced trainer about how far along they really are. You see, it is one thing to sit still in the backyard with no real distractions;

it is quite another matter to stay put in a hunting situation with birds flying, guns going off, and excited hunters moving and shouting. If you are to get the kind of response you want *under any circumstances,* you should introduce a variety of temptations for movement into the training. This takes time.

Start STAY training with your dog sitting at heel. Command STAY, and step around with your right foot so that you are standing facing the dog, and immediately in front of him. In heeling he has come to key off of your left leg, but now you are blocking his path before that leg moves. Eventually, your dog will learn that the right foot lead means STAY and the left foot lead means HEEL. Dogs are very observant.

In obedience trial competition, the handler is allowed to give a hand signal along with the verbal STAY command. He swings the left arm down so that the palm of the left hand is immediately in front of the dog's nose as the command STAY is given. I don't recommend this for the field retriever. It is considered a "threatening gesture," grounds

In obedience trials, you are allowed to give a hand signal and the verbal STAY as you leave your dog. But in all field sports—field trials, hunting tests, and working certificate tests—the hand signal is (rightly, methinks) considered a "threatening gesture," thus is a big NO-NO. In other words, don't do this! Here Mary Jo Gallagher demonstrates the obedience trial hand signal with her Flat-Coat, Fortune.

for immediate elimination, in all formal retriever field activities.

If you step immediately in front of your dog with a right foot lead as you command STAY, he won't be able to move. Now, stand there, praising the pooch, and occasionally repeating the word STAY. You want the dog to associate that word with immobility, so you repeat it while he sits there. You also want to let the dog know you are pleased even though he isn't doing anything, so you praise him. If the beast attempts to move, command NO, reposition him, and repeat the STAY—then resume praising.

What constitutes a move that should be corrected? Personally, I feel you should allow normal head movements, but not any movement of the feet or rump. Not even slight shiftings. If you never allow them, your bright young retriever never has to wonder how much he can get away with.

After a few moments of standing in front of your dog, move back to the heel position. Praise again, then heel him around awhile. Try the STAY two or three times in each session.

After the dog has demonstrated that he understands what STAY means under these ideal conditions, move a little farther away when you step around in front. Continue to step directly in front, right foot first, but then back up a few feet. If the dog moves, correct him. Actually, this is a good time for your youngster to make mistakes, while you are close enough to make quick corrections.

Next, with the dog still on lead, step off with the right foot as you command STAY, but don't step right in front of the dog. Instead, walk straight ahead to the end of the lead and turn to face the dog. If he remains in place, move a little to one side, and then to the other. Walk back and forth, back and forth. Then, return and praise.

Each time lengthen the distance you go away from the dog, and widen the path you walk to either side. Keep the lead on the dog, but drop it from your hand as you move farther from him. Eventually, you will be able to walk all over the backyard while your dog sits in place. The first few times you go behind him are critical. The animal will be strongly tempted to move around just to be able to see you better, so stay close for a few times. If the dog moves, you will be in a better position to make the correction.

When you can walk all over the backyard while your dog remains in place, eliminate the lead and tempt him a little more. Instead of walking, run. If the dog moves—as it is very likely to do at first—correct quickly and start over. When your retriever can handle this running game, clap your hands, sing, talk loudly, whatever, as you run around the yard. A few corrections and your bright youngster will sit there like granite no matter what you do. Good, but that is just the beginning.

Next, have other members of your family come out and walk, run, and play while your dog is on the STAY command. First on-lead, then off. After that is no longer a problem, have a friend with a *trained* dog come into the yard and heel his dog around the back-yard—at a distance from your dog at first, then closer and closer. There is no need to overdo this. Keep the dogs at least five feet apart. Anything closer is showboating, not training.

When your retriever sits rock-steady through all these distractions, take him to a shopping center. There you can work on his

When commanding STAY, step off with your right foot. This helps the dog understand that he is not to HEEL. The right foot lead reinforces the STAY command just as the left foot lead reinforces HEEL. Here Mary Jo Gallagher demonstrates this with her Flat-Coat, Fortune. *Nota bene:* She is *not* giving Fortune the obedience trial hand signal.

heeling as well as the STAY. Of course, do not put the animal in a position where people will run into him or step on his feet. Just their presence is all the distraction you need. Keep him on-lead all the time, and when you make a correction, do it firmly but quietly. Some people who are unfamiliar with dog training may misunderstand if you are too loud or rough.

After all this, your dog has completed his basic training in STAY. It only remains for you to use the command frequently, and insist on absolute obedience every time. If your dog moves, correct him quickly and convincingly, even if it is inconvenient. I have seen trainers leave their dogs in a STAY while teaching hand signals, and allow the dog to creep several feet as they walked away. Too often such a trainer only commands STAY again from a distance, instead of taking the dog back to the original position and correcting the error there. The dog soon learns that he can creep and that the distance he can safely creep depends on how far away the handler is. This frustrating habit can be more easily prevented than cured.

COME-IN

Next to SIT, this command is the most important for bringing your dog under control.

You will eventually use the three commands, RELEASE, SIT, and COME-IN, to control your retriever when hunting in the uplands. You RELEASE him to let him hunt. If he gets too far ahead, you stop him with the SIT whistle and make him wait until you catch up. If he gets too far to either side, you bring him back with the COME-IN whistle, again RELEASEing him when he is within gun range. If the dog doesn't obey these three commands, your days in the uplands will be frustrating, birdless, and probably devoid of much human or canine company.

You should teach COME-IN by both voice and whistle. Over the dog's life, you will use the whistle signal more often. In a day's shoot, you could get hoarse shouting COME-IN every time your dog swings too wide. Tooting the whistle is easier. Then, too, your dog can hear the whistle at a greater distance.

The COME-IN whistle can serve you well around home, too. At least twice a day I let my dogs out of their runs into the (fenced) backyard for a romp. Occasionally one of the gates is open by mistake and my dogs take off for an adventure. When they do, one of my neighbors calls and says that he just saw my "herd" heading south (north, east, or west). I grab a whistle lanyard, go out into the yard and start blowing the COME-IN call. In a few minutes, they come trotting back from wherever. That is so much easier than getting in the car and driving all over the neighborhood looking for them, shouting their names periodically, as I have seen others with untrained dogs do.

The whistle signal that has been almost universally adopted by retrieverites for COME-IN is one long followed by two short toots. TWEEEEEEEEET-TWEET-TWEET. It is trilled rather than blasted to further distinguish it from the single, sharp note used for SIT.

Most retrieverites use HEEL as a voice command for COME-IN. This may sound strange, but it has some logic. When you call your dog to you, you want him to come in and sit down beside you in the heeling position.

You can start teaching COME-IN using the command HEEL as soon as your dog understands the automatic sit while heeling. However, you cannot complete this training until your dog obeys STAY very well. How can you call your dog to you if you cannot first leave him and walk away without being followed?

Initially, start each heeling lesson with your dog sitting in front of you, facing you. Command HEEL and walk at an angle past your dog. He should turn into the heeling position as you pass. At first, you may have to guide him with a few jerk-and-releases, but he should catch on quickly.

Next, command HEEL and delay a second or so before you start walking. If necessary, give a few jerk-and-releases to encourage the dog to get up and come around to the heeling position. Gradually increase the pause between the command and your movement, until the dog is coming all the way around to heel before you start moving.

When your dog is competent at STAY—really solid, not still a bit shaky—leave him in a STAY, walk away a few paces, and command HEEL. Have the lead on, in case the dog is confused and fails to come to you. Use gentle jerk-and-releases if necessary, but nothing rough. If the dog doesn't come voluntarily, he is probably not sure whether HEEL is a command to be obeyed or another distraction thrown in to tempt him to break the STAY. Eventually, he will understand that other commands can override STAY, but at first there may be some confusion and reluctance.

As the dog gathers confidence, move farther away before you command HEEL. Eventually, you should be able to call the dog to you anywhere in the yard with HEEL. One caution: If you call your dog to you every time you leave him in a STAY, you will damage his reliability on STAY. For this reason, you should only call him to you with HEEL about once in every four or five STAYs.

When your retriever will come to you on HEEL from all over the yard, start teaching him to respond to the whistle signal. Initially, command HEEL, and as the dog comes to you, blow the COME-IN whistle signal. He will make the association quickly, especially if you have used this whistle signal in your play retrieving, as recommended in Chapter Two.

After your youngster understands the whistle signal for COME-IN, use it most of the time. You will find it more useful in any hunting situation—easier on your vocal cords and audible at a greater distance. Besides, the human voice frightens birds more surely than does the whistle.

DOWN

DOWN means to lie down, to drop, normally from a sitting position. An optional command, one I have occasionally omitted for the life of a retriever, it nevertheless has its uses. Sometimes, in duck hunting, your retriever is less conspicuous lying than sitting by the blind. Even around the house, you can usually keep him on a STAY command longer in the down position.

Start out with your dog sitting on-lead as you kneel in front of him. Command DOWN, grab both of his front legs near the feet, and pull them straight towards you. He cannot avoid lying down when you do this. Praise him just as if he has done something wonderful as soon as his belly hits the ground.

Place one hand on his withers to prevent him from rising. Continue kneeling. Repeat DOWN several times and praise him often.

After a few moments, step beside him, command HEEL and walk off.

Repeat this until he lies down without help when you command DOWN. Then, stand up beside him. If he tries to get up, force him back down, praising him as soon as he is again in place. After he remains down with you standing, command STAY and move a short distance from him. From this point, you just repeat the STAY training process with the dog in this new position.

MISCELLANEOUS

There are many other commands you can teach your dog, some that will be useful in the field or around home, and others that are just entertaining.

I once taught one of our house dogs to ring a little bell whenever she wanted to go outside to relieve herself. This was cute, guests enjoyed it, but my wife objected. She felt that the dog was controlling us, that we had to run to let her out whenever she rang the bell. I'll admit that Misty did get a little overbearing with it. She would ring the bell when I left the house without her, when the kids went out to play, when she was bored, and on and on. At my wife's request, I have never taught another dog to do this.

On the other hand, my wife taught this same dog to track down our kids when they were small. I don't know how she did it, but she only had to identify the kid, and Misty would lead my wife unerringly to that particular child.

When I was a small child, my mother trained our Boston terrier to wake my father or me up in the morning. Mom would be in the kitchen getting breakfast, and at the appropriate time, she would say, "Go get Jim up" or "Go get Jack (Dad) up," and Scrappy would run into the appropriate bedroom and jump right in the middle of the selected victim. There he would lick the face until the feet hit the floor. As I remember, I liked this a lot better than Dad did, but it worked on both of us.

I could go on. However, I am sure you could match me, trick for trick, with the little things you have taught a dog once he acquired the habit of learning. Perhaps this is the most important part of all this obedience training, just getting the dog to enjoy learning.

DOG

HANDLER

Single Marked Retrieves

FROM PLAY-RETRIEVING TO"REAL" RETRIEVING

The transition from the play-retrieving discussed in Chapter Two to "serious" single marked retrieves is a gradual process involving the following steps: introducing throwers (assistants who throw dummies and birds for your dog), lengthening out on bare ground, gun-proofing, steadying, introducing birds, moving into cover, starting water work, and decoy-proofing. In some ways, these steps flow and blend, rather than remain separate sequential capsules. For example, you can (and should) introduce birds while you are still steadying the pup.

Still, each step has its own general prerequisites. You cannot successfully introduce a thrower until you have completed play-retrieving. You cannot lengthen your pup's retrieves until you introduce the thrower. You cannot gun-proof him until you lengthen his retrieves. And so on.

Moreover, there is one general prerequisite for all of them: *You must know how to handle your dog.* Your own actions can make his job easier or more difficult. So, before we talk about what you will teach your dog, let's talk about what you should do and should not do as a handler.

Initially, your young retriever needs all the help you can give him. Later, after he understands his job, you can introduce the subtleties of actual hunting, field trial, and hunting tests—sitting beside the blind or on a beaver dam, hidden throwers, you pointing and shooting a gun, and so on.

This is KISS (Keep It Simple, Stupid) handling on a single mark. Sit your dog facing the thrower, then let your dog lock in on the thrower before calling for the throw. Watch your dog, not the thrower. If you don't watch your dog, you cannot know where he is looking. Here Mary Jo Gallagher sets her Flat-Coat, Fortune up for a single, while Marilyn Corbin (across the pond) acts as thrower.

For now, follow the KISS system (Keep It Simple, Stupid). Heel your pup on-lead to the "line" (starting point). Once there, face the clearly visible thrower. Only signal for the throw when your dog is sitting at heel concentrating on the thrower. Always use the belt cord, even before you steady him.

EQUIPMENT

As you progress from puppy retrieving to the real thing, you need several new items of equipment: a belt cord, a blank pistol, several dummies, and birds (pigeons, ducks, and perhaps pheasants).

Belt cord: This is a short length of cord about the size found on venetian blinds. Its purpose is to allow you to control your youngster at the line before you release him to retrieve. Eventually, you use it to steady him. It should be about 36" long with a loop on one end (to attach to your belt). The other end should be plain. I prefer nylon because I can burn the ends to prevent raveling.

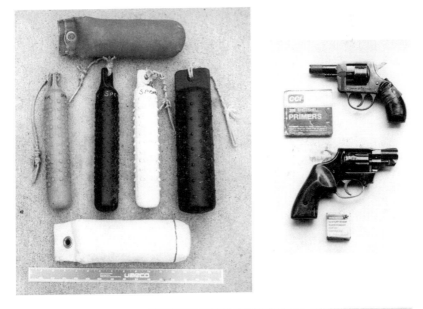

Top: This is the belt cord, shown here with a whistle and lanyard to indicate the length and thickness of the belt cord. The cord should be about 3' long and preferably made of nylon. Note that both ends of the cord have been burned to prevent raveling.

Left: A variety of dummies, with a 15" ruler to help visualize the sizes. At top and bottom are canvas dummies. In the middle are plastic "knobbies" in three colors (orange, black, white, black) and two sizes.

Right: At top is a .32 caliber blank revolver that has been converted to shoot the less expensive shotshell primers (shown by gun). Below is a regular snub-nosed .22 caliber revolver with a box of .22 blank shells.

Blank pistol: I prefer a .32 pistol which has been modified to accept inexpensive 12 gauge primers. If you cannot find a mail order catalog that offers them, you might contact your gunsmith to see if he could make one up for you from an old .32 pistol. (A .22 won't work because 12 gauge primers require center-fire).

Many use .22 starter pistols or old regular .22 pistols with blank cartridges. They do everything you need done, but the shells cost over a nickel apiece these days (compared to less than two cents apiece for primers).

You should avoid the cheap little pistols that fire only .22 crimp shells. Those don't make enough noise for retriever work, where the gun is normally fired some distance from the dog.

Dummies: You need a number of full-sized dummies. I prefer the plastic knobbies in both sizes and at least two colors (white and red). A minimum set would include six small whites, six small reds, three large whites, and three large reds. That will get you by for single marked retrieves. However, when you start doing doubles, you need a lot more. If you do marks with too few dummies, you have to resupply your thrower too often, eating up time that could be better spent training dogs.

Birds: Check with other dog trainers in your area to find out where you can buy pigeons, ducks, and pheasants.

In retriever training, you can re-use birds many times. Just freeze and thaw them between uses. You can save a lot of money on pigeons by scavenging at the fun trials conducted in your area for pointing and flushing breeds. They use only live birds, and have to dispose of the dead carcasses. Generally, they are grateful to anyone who will take them off their hands.

One little note on birds: I have delayed their introduction into your program until you start steadying your pup for one reason: If you tried them earlier and your dog reacted badly, it would worry you too much. Now that he is retrieving dummies quite well, you won't panic if he doesn't love the first pigeon you show him.

INTRODUCING A THROWER
You can't throw a dummy far enough to bring out the real potential of a retriever. Besides, in steadying and most other training beyond

puppy stuff, you need to concentrate on your dog. You can't do that if you do your own throwing. Thus, you need an assistant from now on. Fortunately, so does every other retriever trainer in your area, so you shouldn't have much difficulty in setting up a training group in which members take turns throwing for each other.

Before introducing a thrower, you should have established yourself as a "secondary lair" to which your youngster brings the dummy. To test for this, position yourself some distance from his primary lair and toss the dummy right at it. If the pup picks the dummy up and whirls to bring it to you, you have succeeded. If he so much as hesitates, he needs more work in play-retrieving.

The introduction of the thrower should take place in your backyard, where you have done the pup's play-retrieving. You should use only short retrieves and white dummies. You are introducing the thrower, not trying to give your pup a challenging retrieve. Have your pup sit at heel facing the thrower. Naturally, he doesn't know what that "other guy" is doing out there, so he may ignore him. Thus, when you signal for the throw, the thrower should holler "Hey! Hey! Hey!" to get the dog's attention before throwing the dummy.

He should toss the dummy in a nice high arc so that it falls about fifteen or twenty yards from him (the thrower). Figure 1 shows the proper angles for throws. The dummy should never be thrown straight at or straight away from the dog and handler, for either will encourage the dog to run to the thrower instead of to the dummy.

Let your pup break to retrieve, but give the command to retrieve as he does. When he picks up the dummy, blow the come-in whistle and encourage him to return.

At first your pup may try to deliver the dummy to the thrower. Till now, you have done the throwing and your dog has returned the dummy to you. Now, someone else is throwing, so...

Some pups learn the correct procedure—always bringing the dummy to you—easily. For these, you only need blow the come-in whistle, run away, and clap your hands during his first few returns.

Other pups grasp this concept slowly. You can speed such a youngster's understanding by making the thrower inaccessible, like in a pickup bed or on the other side of a wire fence. My backyard has a four-foot chain-link fence around it. I send my thrower into an

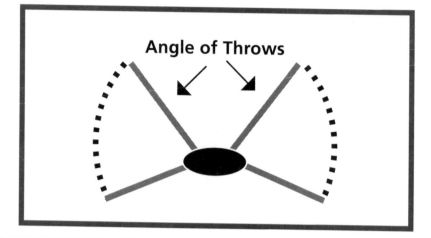

Angle of Throws

FIG.1: Reasonable angles for throw

Your thrower should keep the throws within the angles shown here. Your dog can learn to mark throws within these angles, but not those outside them. Throws angled back more sharply look, to the dog, as if they were thrown straight up. Throws angled in more sharply encourage young dogs to hunt short, a bad habit to start. A more experienced dog cannot tell throws angled in more from similar throws angled back.

adjacent property, from which he tosses the dummy into my yard. The dog learns that he cannot deliver to the thrower because of the fence, so he harkens to my incessant whistling and clapping.

Years ago I took a friend who was unfamiliar with dog work along on a pheasant hunt. We had my dog with us, and naturally she had been trained to retrieve every bird to me. On the way out, I told my friend that he and I might shoot at the same bird occasionally and not know who really hit it. "Don't worry, though," I told him, "Misty here can always tell who hit the bird, and she will deliver it to that person—every time. Amazing dog, really." He was completely taken in until Misty brought me a bird that I hadn't shot at. Then, my friend gave me a loud rundown on his interpretation of my genealogy.

One more thing about throwers: they should stand still before and after the throw, facing the direction of the throw. During this early backyard work, the dog would probably not become confused by a moving thrower—since the dummy is in plain sight—but later, when you work him in cover, especially on multiple marks, he would have difficulty remembering his mark if the thrower moved around. Eventually, if you are interested in any of the hunting tests, you will set up retrieves in which the throwers are hidden. If you are interested in field trials, you will set up "retiring gun" tests, in which the throwers hide after the throw. However, nowhere will you be required to set up retrieves in which visible throwers move around.

This seemingly minor accomplishment—retrieving to you when someone else throws—sets up all of the dog's future work in marked retrieves. It may be simple, but it is not trivial.

LENGTHENING THE RETRIEVES

Next, you should extend the distances your dog is expected to retrieve. Your initial goal should be to lengthen him out to 100 yards or so on bare ground, where he has no difficulty locating the dummy. Incidentally, when I speak of "bare ground," I mean any place where the dummy remains in sight—bare ground, clipped grass, etc.

You may be tempted to go straight from the backyard to cover. After all, you plan to hunt this dog in cover, don't you? However, he will progress more rapidly if you attack one problem at a time. Let him become comfortable with length on bare ground before moving into cover.

I made the mistake of combining the introduction to length with the introduction to cover once. "Hustler" was a big, good-looking golden retriever of my own Rumrunner breeding. His owner joined my training group after the other dogs were already in cover. Thus, we started Hustler there rather than taking him back to bare ground, as we should have. He failed to find the dummy often, especially at distances of over 50 yards. Too many failures discouraged this very sensitive dog. Eventually, he refused to retrieve. We had to go back to short, simple retrieves to rekindle his interest and rebuild his confidence. We spent much more time curing the problem than we would have preventing it.

You can teach your dog more than just length in these initial drills. For example, if you change locations often, he will develop confidence

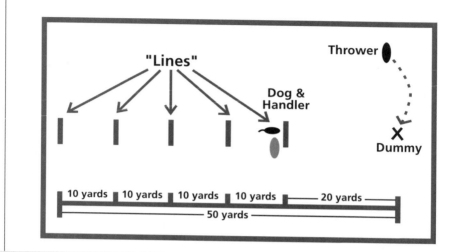

FIG. 2: Lengthening out drill
To lengthen your youngster's marks out on bare ground, set up a 20 yard single. As your dog goes after it, you should run back 10 or 15 yards. When he delivers to you, rerun the test from there (now 30 to 35 yards). As he goes after the dummy, again run back 10 to 15 yards. When he delivers to you rerun the test from there (now 40 to 50 yards). And so on out to whatever maximum length you have selected. Your dog will never fail, so will develop confidence in his ability to complete long retrieves.

in his ability to handle new territory, which will be valuable when you move into cover. Further, if you have several different people act as throwers, your dog will learn to ignore the thrower and go after the dummy.

Figure 2 shows how the lengthening out process is done. Position the thrower in one place (and have him make every throw the same). Then, establish three "lines" (positions from which you start a retrieve), the first about 20 yards from the thrower, the second about 35 yards, and the third about 50 yards.

The thrower should have at least six white dummies. That way, he will need to replenish his supply only between dogs, which saves a lot of time. The dummies should be in a container at his feet or in the game bag of his vest. Either way, the pup will not be distracted by their scent.

Heel your youngster on the belt cord to the line at 20 yards. When the pup "locks in" (focuses his attention on the thrower), signal for the throw. As he breaks, give your command to retrieve. With a white dummy on bare ground, he should run right to it. As he does, you should run back to the next line (35 yards). That way, when he brings the dummy to you, he will not even notice that his next retrieve is almost twice as long as the one he has just completed.

Signal for another throw from the 35 yard line. As your pup sails after it, run back to the 50 yard line. When he brings the dummy to you, have him do a few retrieves from there.

In one lesson, you have stretched your dog out from backyard distances to 50 yards. In the next session, you can set the closest line at 35 yards, the middle one at 50, and the far one at 70 yards. In each session the lengths should be increased until 100 yards is no problem to the dog. All through this process, you should change locations frequently.

After your dog can handle 100 yard retrieves on bare ground with white dummies in several locations, shorten up a bit and change to red dummies. Dogs are color-blind, so red dummies blend in with the ground. Start out at about 50 yards, and add length as your dog develops confidence with dummies that are not readily visible.

Throughout this process, do not leave the dummies he delivers to you on the ground, where they could interfere with a subsequent retrieve. Wear a hunting vest and stuff them in your gamebag. That way, they neither inconvenience you nor interfere with your dog.

GUN-PROOFING

Once your dog can handle 100 yard retrieves on bare ground with red dummies, you should gun-proof him. This is so simple with retrievers—compared to bird-dogs—that the experienced bird-dog trainer with his first retriever cannot believe there isn't more to it. The secret lies in getting the dog to associate the sound of the gun with something pleasant, namely retrieving.

To do this, set up a 100 yard retrieve, still on bare ground, and use white dummies. When you signal for a throw, the thrower should yell "Hey! Hey! Hey!" as usual, but then should fire a .22 blank shell before he throws. At 100 yards the noise is minimal, so the pup should make the retrieve with no problem. Then, move closer, say 75 yards. This time the thrower should not yell, but should just shoot before throwing. In no time, your dog will associate the sound of the gun with a dummy flying. From then on, you only need to move slowly closer until the pup has no problem with a .22 blank at 10 or 15 yards. That may take a couple of sessions. Then move back to 100 yards and introduce a 20 gauge the same way. Save the big 12 for later, after the pup is handling birds in cover.

Hereafter, the thrower should shoot—normally a .22 blank for economic reasons—before each throw instead of yelling. Gunfire becomes music to your dog, for it tells him he is about to make a retrieve.

STEADYING

Your young retriever has learned to do retrieves out to 100 yards, and loves the sound of the gun. Before you move him into cover, you should do two more things on bare ground: Steady him, and introduce him to birds. You can do these two in parallel, with some of each in each training session. This section describes the steadying process and the next tells how to introduce birds.

Why should steadying be done on bare ground? To eliminate all problems not directly associated with the steadying process. If you were to steady your pup in cover, he would fail to find the dummy too often. A dog that is struggling to break just cannot mark a fall. If that fall is in cover, he probably will not find it. This is a problem you just don't need at this time. If you steady on bare ground with white dummies, he will complete every retrieve, no matter how tangled you and he get as he struggles to break and you struggle to restrain him.

The secret of using the belt cord effectively lies in leaving it slack as the pup sits beside you. The slack belt cord doesn't let the animal feel your control until he tries to break. Then, it snubs him quickly. The dog comes to believe that some mysterious force prevents him from breaking. Similarly, since the dog doesn't feel the slack cord loosen as you give the command to retrieve, he comes to feel that your command removes the mysterious force.

If you hold the cord tight, the dog can feel physical restraint before he attempts to break. He can also feel it slacken when you send him to retrieve. He thus learns to remain steady as long as he can feel the restraint, and to break when it disappears. This is definitely not

To use a belt cord effectively, leave slack in it as the dog sits beside you. That way he feels no pressure—unless he tries to break. Here Marilyn Corbin demonstrates proper belt cord use with her young golden, Summer.

what you want. You should teach the dog that only your command releases him. The belt cord absolutely must be slack to do its job.

Many trainers use the command STAY as a steadying command. For a dog that has been properly steadied with the belt cord, that is unnecessary. Such a dog has learned that only the command to retrieve allows him the freedom to go, so STAY is superfluous.

Not only that, but those who use STAY that way cannot later use it effectively to control their honoring dog. Honoring—sitting while another dog works—is required in the advanced stakes of field trials and hunting tests, as well as being handy in many hunting situations. STAY is ideal as an indication to the dog that he will honor instead of retrieve—provided it is not used to steady the dog before he is sent to retrieve.

You could make a case that the handler lies to his dog when he commands STAY and then sends him to retrieve. STAY should mean "Just sit there, Buster; you aren't going anywhere this time." The person who commands STAY just to kid his dog into sticking around until sent won't fool the animal long. STAY will quickly lose all meaning—as does any often-repeated lie.

Until now, you have allowed your youngster to break as the dummy was thrown. However, you gave the command to retrieve as he sailed away. You did this so he would associate that command with the act of leaving to retrieve. Now, you make that association stronger by teaching the dog that he cannot leave until he hears that word.

Start out by setting up a simple bare ground retrieve of about 40 yards, using a white dummy. Attach the belt cord to your belt and loop the end through your dog's collar. Hold the loop with your left hand, allowing plenty of slack.

Signal for the throw, and brace yourself. As the dog breaks, jerk him rudely back into position, saying NO! HEEL! From now on, you will use these words (followed by a few optional expletives) to control the occasional break every dog makes, so accustom him to them now.

Summer has tried to break, and Marilyn Corbin is controlling her with the belt cord—using both hands because she is small and Summer is very strong.

The first few retrieves can be hectic for both of you. The dog may stand up and claw the air. He may flip over on his back or he may tangle the belt cord around your legs. No matter what happens—even if you wind up on the ground with him—get him back sitting in the heel position before giving him the command to retrieve. With the white dummy lying there on bare ground, he cannot fail to make the retrieve.

After a few sessions, when he shows that he has begun to grasp this strange new idea of yours, you can pause longer and longer before releasing him. Don't get ridiculous about this. Four or five seconds is plenty. Actually, it is more important that you vary the time between the fall and the magic word than it is that you lengthen it very much. You should sometimes send him quickly, other times make him wait longer. Don't let him establish a rhythm, as he would if you always sent him on a count of two (or three or whatever).

Some people give a signal with their left hand along with the command to retrieve. Personally, I feel that if the dog is properly locked in on the dummy, this is superfluous, even distracting. Later, in multiple marks, you may want to use your left hand to steady the dog's concentration when he is a bit confused, and you will certainly use it in blind retrieves. However, for now, just send him with the verbal command—when he is locked in on the fall.

Of course, you can tell when your pup is locked in and ready only if you look at him before you send him. Watch the fall until it hits the ground, but then turn your complete attention to your dog. This is much like the "keep your head down" maxim in golf.

Vary the length of the retrieves during this process, from very short to 100 yards. The short ones offer the greatest temptation to break. The longer ones build his confidence. When he was allowed to break, he may have covered 20 to 25 yards while the dummy was in the air, so his 100 yard retrieves were really only 75 or 80 yards. Now, they are a full 100 yards.

When he no longer struggles to break, switch to red dummies, still on bare ground. These offer less visual aid, but on bare ground, they are still readily seen when the dog gets close to them. However, even after you are absolutely sure your dog will not break, continue to use the belt cord. I personally see no reason to stop using it until the dog is well along in double marked retrieves. There is no prize for being the first in your group to stop using the belt cord, and there can be some real problems if you take it off too soon. Why take the risk?

INTRODUCING BIRDS

You can introduce birds in parallel with the steadying process, and eventually merge the two—use birds in your single marks on bare ground to tempt your pup to break.

You should first introduce him to a dead pigeon. Pigeons are available almost everywhere. They are cheap, at least compared to ducks or pheasants. They give off an attractive scent, and they are small enough for any pup to handle.

Start just as you did with dummies: Let the dog smell and mouth the pigeon while you hold it. His initial reaction may be anything from wild enthusiasm to fear. If he is too enthusiastic—too rough with the bird—start over with a frozen pigeon. If he sinks a tooth in that one, he will get a very unpleasant sensation, as you can imagine.

If he shows fear, don't try to force the bird into his mouth. Perhaps the best retriever I have ever owned—old Duffy—was afraid of birds of any kind until he was over one year old. Yet because he had a strong retrieving instinct, was very stylish, and had a big water entry, I kept working him on dummies...and hoping. I gave him frequent opportunities with dead pigeons, but allowed him to adjust at his own speed. Finally, when he was twelve or thirteen months old, he became very birdy. Perhaps he would have come around sooner if I had tried just a pigeon wing. That sometimes works.

The typical retriever pup loves the pigeon from the first, but handles it gently. If yours is like that, go through the same preliminary play-retrieving you used with dummies.

If you had any sort of return problem with dummies, you will probably have one with pigeons, too. Even if you had no problem with dummies, your dog may show more possessiveness with the bird and be reluctant to bring it to you. Go quickly to the rope and stay with it until you win the argument. Hustler, the golden mentioned before, never refused to return with a dummy, but gave us quite a time with birds. Even after he seemed reliable, we had him drag a twenty-foot rope for several weeks so we could catch him more easily.

Once your dog is doing good work with pigeons in the backyard, use them instead of dummies in his bare ground work. You can freeze dead pigeons between uses, then thaw and reuse them many times before they become unfit. This is also true of ducks and pheasants. However, there are limits to this. I once used a particular dead duck too long—until my dog rolled on it instead of retrieving it one day, which told me it had become too ripe.

You should also introduce your dog to "shot fliers" with live pigeons. This takes three helpers, one to throw and two to shoot the bird. Of course, you should be sure that your dog is completely gun-proofed before trying this. Even then, set the initial shot fliers up at 75 to 100 yards. Stay on bare ground, where your pup has no difficulty finding the downed bird.

After he is comfortable with pigeons introduce him to pheasants and ducks. The process is the same with each bird. However, some dogs are intimidated by these larger birds. If yours shies away that way, here is a trick that usually works: Remove the bird's entrails, legs, wings, head and neck, but leave the feathers in place. That reduces its size and weight substantially. Most dogs that are comfortable with pigeons take to the larger bird in this condition.

MOVING INTO COVER

Your dog is now steady and can handle bare ground retrieves out to 100 yards. You can now start him in cover—provided you have properly introduced him to cover (per the instructions in Chapter Two).

I remember a female golden I helped a man train many years ago. She did very well in basic obedience and bare ground retrieving, but she was a house dog that had never been exposed to anything rougher than a shag rug. When we tried to get her to retrieve in cover, she just looked at us as if to say, "Surely, you don't expect dainty little ME to go into that strange-smelling grass before you mow it, do you?" We had to interrupt her training for a couple of weeks to give her daily romps in cover before we could proceed. She went on to become a real cover-busting retriever after that.

The scents found in cover can distract a dog at first, and make it impossible for him to make a decent retrieve. Many a new member brought a young retriever to the training sessions we used to hold at the Jayhawk Retriever Club lease on Saturday mornings, only to find that the dog was more interested in the new scents than in retrieving. Typically, the dog had been working nicely in the backyard, and the owner was anxious to show everyone what this young marvel could do. The dog would start out for the mark, but would get sidetracked by some fascinating scent along the way. This surprised—and sometimes angered—the owner. Even then, it was often difficult to persuade such a person to take his dog for romps in cover until all the new scents were familiar before trying to get him to retrieve there.

In bare ground work, your only real concern has been distance. That is only one dimension in cover work, where you must also be concerned about terrain variations, cover variations, and wind direction. Actually, distance is the least important factor in cover.

However, it is better to keep the distances short while introducing the other factors. Give your dog plenty of short retrieves in all sorts of cover and terrain, and add distance gradually. In cover he may fail to find the dummy or bird. If he fails too often, especially at first, he may become discouraged and lose interest in retrieving. Trial and success can teach him more and faster than trial and error.

You can use two techniques to minimize failures: reruns and "salting."

You should rerun your dog on every mark he doesn't "step on" or "pin" (do perfectly). This not only gives him confidence, in that he will surely succeed the second time even if he failed initially, but it also develops his marking ability. The first time he runs the test, he finds out where the dummy is (even if he has been helped); in the rerun he sees the fall from the line again while knowing exactly where the dummy is falling. It's like sighting-in a rifle.

The rerun is important throughout the training process: single marks, multiple marks, blind retrieves, and combination marked and blind retrieves. In fact, I have often commented that the three R's of retriever training are: Rerun, Rerun, Rerun.

"Salting"—scattering several dummies in the area of the intended

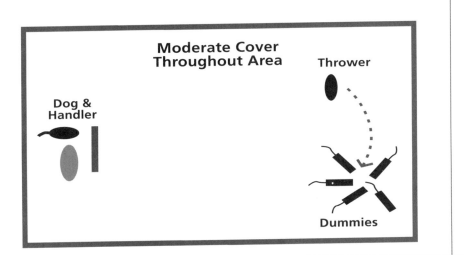

Moderate Cover Throughout Area

Thrower

Dog & Handler

Dummies

fall before you run your dog—can also be helpful at first. If the pup gets to the area, he will find one of those dummies. Occasionally, a dog picks up two dummies, or drops one and picks up another. A little of this is nothing serious, but it should not be encouraged, so discontinue salting as soon as possible.

Never salt with pigeons. If the dog picks up two pigeons, he may mash one, which could start hardmouth.

Even with salting, your dog will sometimes fail to find the dummy. When that happens, you have only two choices: You can signal the thrower to help your dog out, or you can walk out there and help him yourself. I prefer the former, for I have had two dogs that decided that they shouldn't even leave the line without me after I helped them a few times. That is a nasty problem to deal with, and should be avoided. I have never had a problem with a dog that has been helped exclusively by the thrower.

Give your dog every opportunity to find the dummy on his own. As long as he is hunting aggressively, even if he is some distance from the area of the fall, leave him alone. Often he will work things out for himself, which will do much for his confidence.

FIG. 3: "Salting," a technique to improve marking
To build your dog's confidence in cover, have your thrower "salt" the area of the fall with a few dummies before he makes the first throw. That way, if your dog drives all the way to the area of the fall, he will find a dummy rather quickly.

However, when he shows you that he can't find it, either by returning toward you or by wandering off disinterestedly, you should immediately signal the thrower to help him out. The thrower should walk to the dummy, pick it up, holler "Hey! Hey! Hey!" and toss it straight up, so it lands at his (the thrower's) feet. If the dog doesn't see it that time, the thrower should do it again—and again, if necessary. The dummy should always land where it originally fell, so the dog will have it properly located when he is rerun.

Every pup eventually figures out that the thrower has a bunch of dummies at his feet. To the young dog the logic of getting one there instead of hunting for the mark is overwhelming. Training must overcome this logic or a frustrating habit will set in. Some dogs catch on if the thrower yells "No! Get!" or something like that. Others need to be touched lightly with a whip. I prefer to have the thrower stand still and swing the whip around, so the dog is only hit if he insists on coming too close. The thrower should never chase the dog.

As your youngster works through these problems, gradually lengthen his retrieves and incorporate various hazards with the cover, terrain, and wind. Wind can be tricky. Downwind retrieves are to be preferred because they force the dog to drive deeper to scent the bird. Cross-winds away from the thrower make most tests easier, since the dog only needs to swing a little wide to use his nose. Cross-winds into the thrower complicate things because they tempt the dog to run behind the thrower where scent from the dummy sack can confuse the pup. Upwind retrieves encourage the dog to quarter out to the bird, a bad habit that is easier to prevent than to cure. Therefore, never give a young pup upwind retrieves. Never.

Generally, you should rerun every test the dog doesn't "pin." However, there is one exception: the shot flier. The second one would normally not fall very close to where the pup picked up the first one. Thus, a rerun would confuse a young dog rather than help his marking.

RETRIEVING IN WATER

Water work should lag behind land work throughout your training program for several reasons. First, water is a more difficult medium.

Second, you cannot easily correct mistakes there. Third, your pup should develop a good attitude towards water from the start, so he should be very successful there.

His initial water retrieves should follow closely after his introduction to swimming (see Chapter Two). As soon as he shows that he enjoys swimming, you can start tossing puppy dummies a few feet in the drink for him. Keep them short. Keep them fun. Keep him successful.

By the time he is well into his bare ground work, before you steady him, he should be doing short water retrieves that you throw for him.

Introduce him to the thrower in water only after he returns to you instead of to the thrower on land. However, don't lengthen his retrieves as rapidly in the water as you have on land. If you rush him along faster than he is ready to go, he will eventually refuse to enter the water. When that happens, you have two choices, both bad: You can accept his decision not to retrieve, and let a refusing habit start; or you can force him in some manner, and start a bad attitude towards water. Any refusal at this point is a lose-lose proposition, so don't press him any faster than he seems willing to go. Very important.

Another thing that will help prevent refusals is plenty of praise from you when the dog reaches the dummy. Let him know you are pleased, and he will want to repeat the performance.

At first, your dog's delivery will probably not be too good. He will want to stop as soon as he is out of the water, drop the dummy and shake the water out of his coat. You will eventually solve this by force-breaking him. For now, there are two stop-gap ways of dealing with this: Start running the other way as soon as he gets to the shore, and shout encouragement to him to follow you; or meet him at the edge of the water and take the dummy before he can drop it. Above all, don't show any disapproval of his delivery, no matter how bad. He must think water is more fun than anything, so any displeasure from you is counter-productive.

However, you should be concerned about another delivery problem, if it occurs. Some dogs return near shore and stop to play with the dummy instead of bringing it to you. Cindy, a golden retriever bitch that belonged to my oldest daughter years ago, had this problem. She would swim any distance to get the dummy, then return near enough to shore to get her feet on the bottom. There she would toss the dummy in the air, slap at it with her front paws, grab it, spin around—over and over again. No amount of coaxing, commanding, or tooting of the whistle fazed her. I was unable to convince my daughter that she should put a rope on Cindy, so we never solved the problem. With any kind of luck, I will do better with you.

First off, completely cure any return problem on land before asking the dog to retrieve in water. Then, if he refuses to leave the water, put the rope on him and force him to come to you, with or without the dummy. Do this until he has no thought of playing games with you. If you eliminate the rope too soon, the dog will learn that he has to return when it is on and can do as he damned well pleases when it is not. The only sensible thing to do is use the rope until there is no doubt about his return in water.

Now, back to the dogs that either have no return problem or have had it cured. If your dog is still beating the water with his front feet as he swims, keep his retrieves short until he overcomes this. Some waterbeaters keep knocking the dummy under water with their paws as they try to grab it. Rumrunner's B&B was such a dog. She would swim to the dummy, reach for it, but knock it under the surface with her front feet before she could get it. Then, she would swim around in circles looking for it. It would pop up, and she would repeat the same routine. Fortunately, she was persistent and always came back with the dummy. Some dogs will give up more easily so the thrower should be positioned where he can assist such a dog.

Frequently, a pup beats the water on the way to the dummy and then swims properly on the return. Once he starts this, it is only a short time until he will swim properly all the time.

After he is over the water-beating, you may safely start toughening his water marks up a bit. There are two dimensions to this process: length and cover.

It is safer to work on length first, and save cover until after the dog is very comfortable with fairly long water retrieves, say 75 yards, and has been steadied. Always use large white dummies as you lengthen his water retrieves. Their visibility will prevent him from giving up part way there, another form of refusal.

What should you do if your dog does refuse? Normally, with a young retriever, you should admit you overtaxed him, back up a few steps, and try to prevent another refusal.

Set up all of these early water marks so your pup will not be tempted to run the bank, going or coming. Later, you will have to decide whether to "water-force" your dog to take angled entries, and to stay on a straight line to and from every fall. He is not ready for that training now, so avoid all bank running situations.

During this lengthening process in water you will probably start steadying your retriever in his land work. Since you can't allow him to break in water while insisting that he be steady on land, you should interrupt the lengthening process in water, go back to short water retrieves, and do the steadying on both land and water simultaneously. Once this is completed, you can resume lengthening your dog's marks in water.

When your dog is retrieving in open water out to about 75 yards and loving it, you should start introducing cover work in water.

There are three different cover situations: cover in the water where the dummy falls; cover in the water between the line and the fall; and falls on land (in cover) across water.

The last is the easiest to set up, but the least beneficial to the retriever. You see, if the dog becomes convinced that the dummy is always on land, he will run the bank. Most of your water marks should fall in the water rather than across it on land. An occasional land-water-land retrieve is fine, but don't overdo it. In a field trial, I saw a dog swim right past a shackled duck (back when those were legal) in open water and hunt the shore. This dog had apparently had so few marks in the water that he swam past the duck with his "hunting switch" turned off.

Throw as many marks in cover in water as possible. However, initially make sure that your thrower can help your dog out if he fails to find the dummy. This means sloshing around in the pond, something everyone in your training group must be willing to do.

Cover between the line and the mark is more difficult, so should be added only after the dog is comfortable with retrieves in which the only cover is around the fall. Don't rush things. Remember: *success, success, success*. Every failure in this early water work is a disaster.

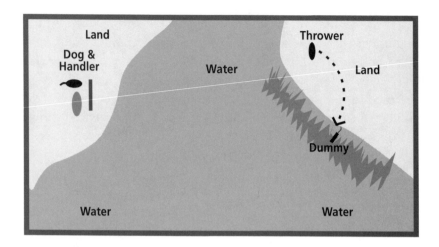

Land

Dog &
Handler

Water

Thrower

Land

Dummy

Water

Water

FIG. 4: Mark thrown in cover in water

As often as you can, have your thrower put the dummy in cover in water rather on land across water. This discourages bank-running, because the dog becomes accustomed to finding dummies in the water.

Shorten up when you start tossing water marks in cover. Let your dog develop confidence in his ability to do the work before making it difficult. Since a dog swims so much slower than he runs, he must remember each water mark much longer than a land mark of equal distance.

One other precaution: If you work your dog in water that has stumps in it—which is a good idea, since you will hunt in such places—make sure there are no underwater stumps in the area where he will enter the water. If a dog takes a long leap as he enters, he could seriously injure himself by landing on a submerged stump. At the very least, he could develop a bad case of water-shyness. If necessary (due to murky water), wade around to be sure his entry area is safe.

Some dogs take naturally to water with cover in it, while others are a bit spooky. I have had one or two that acted like the lake was full of ghosts if there were stumps, brush, and other visible obstructions between the line and the mark. The way to handle this is to stop tossing marks long enough to wade around with your dog in this kind of water and let him get used to it when he is not under any pressure to retrieve. Wade around and praise him for following

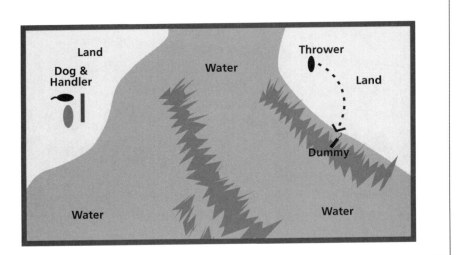

you. Let him know you are pleased, and he will adjust quickly.

INTRODUCING DECOYS

After your pup is doing good work in water with cover, you should teach him to leave decoys alone. You certainly don't want to send him after a strong cripple someday only to have him stop short and bring you a decoy, do you?

Like almost everything else in retriever training, you start this on land. Scatter several decoys around in the backyard. Then, put your dog on lead and heel him around through them. Every time he tries to sniff a decoy, jerk up on the lead and say "No!" After a few corrections, he will ignore them. Then, set up a simple retrieve. Toss a dummy off to one side of the decoy spread and send him for it. If he veers towards the decoys, holler "No!" at him. If he persists, go shake him up and start again.

After he can handle retrieves off to the side, make things a bit tougher—toss the dummy beyond the decoys, so he has to run right through them. Correct him if he even sniffs one as he goes through. Next, toss the dummy right in the middle of the decoys.

FIG. 5: Cover between line and fall in a water test
In water marks, cover in the water between the line and the fall makes the test much more difficult. Inexperienced dogs tend to hunt the first cover they come to rather than driving through it to get to the cover which hides the dummy. If your dog does this at first, have your thrower help him out . . . and then rerun the test.

In teaching your dog to ignore decoys, start on land. Spread a few decoys around, then heel your dog through them. Everytime he tries to nose one, snap the lead and command NO! HEEL! Here Marilyn Corbin heels her young Golden, Summer, through decoys. Summer is becoming too curious about a decoy . . . and is about to be corrected.

When he can handle this bare ground work, move into shallow water. Heel him through the decoys, just as you did in the backyard. Then, toss a dummy off to one side—and so on.

Why not start out in water? You want to correct your dog in water as infrequently as possible, so you do the initial work, when he is most apt to need correction, on land. You take him to sea only when you know he will not need a correction.

After your dog is decoy-proofed, use them in his water marks frequently. Let them become old-hat to him, things that are always there to be ignored. Place them close to the line at first, then further out, and finally near the fall itself.

One thing you should never do in any of your training is use

pigeons in the water, especially pigeons that have been frozen and thawed several times. They are delicate and your retriever could get a mouthful of fresh meat. I have seen several normally soft-mouthed dogs eat a wet pigeon as they swam.

MAKING IT MORE LIKE HUNTING

Until now, you have followed the KISS system of handling—starting every retrieve standing with your pup sitting at heel facing the visible thrower. Now it is time to branch out a bit.

After your dog ignores decoys while being heeled through them, toss a dummy for him to retrieve—first off to the side, then straight across them, and so on. Here Mary Jo Gallagher's Flat-Coat, Fortune, has run through the decoys and is about to pick up a big white dummy.

In actual hunting, you sometimes sit on a stool or in a blind. You can practice both, now that the pup is basically steadied. However, cut yourself a longer belt cord and use it, just in case.

In actual hunting, you do not have a visible thrower for your retriever to key off of. You can now introduce him to hidden throwers and birds that come from nowhere. However, start out by hiding the thrower on reruns only. Let the thrower stand in plain sight in front of a tree or bush for the initial mark, and then have him step behind it for the rerun. If you plan to run hunting tests, you should also have him blow a duck call instead of shooting a .22 blank before he throws. That is a common practice.

In hunting, you point and shoot a shotgun yourself. You can start that now, especially when sitting on a stool during reruns with a hidden thrower. Your pup will quickly learn to look in the direction you point the gun. Incidentally, start out just pointing it, not shooting. After your dog learns the routine of looking where you point, start shooting, too, but only with a 20 gauge at first.

Only after your dog is doing good work on significant singles with KISS handling should you simulate hunting situations. Here pro Omar Driskill shoots from a stool while his dog sits in a little box beside him. Note that he has snapped the dog's collar to the box—to keep him steady. When you first introduce hunting gimmicks, your dog may break, even if he is steady with KISS.

LOOK HOW FAR YOU'VE COME

Retriever training sometimes seems a bit slow. However, it is really like driving in the mountains on those long gradual inclines: You can't see how much you are climbing by looking forward; you have to look in your rearview mirror.

Right now, your puppy has made outstanding progress, and he is probably still quite a ways from his first birthday. He is obedience trained, which alone sets him above most hunting dogs. He is steady. He can handle significant single marks on land and in water. He leaves decoys alone, and he can handle birds. You can take him hunting right now, and he will make you proud of his performance.

What's more, you have become a dog trainer while he was becoming a hunting dog. Not bad for a couple of rookies, eh?

FORCE-BREAKING

WHAT IS IT?

Until now you probably have not been getting consistent delivery to hand from your retriever pup. He sometimes drops the dummy or bird at your feet, either as he approaches you or as he goes to the heel position beside you. In fact, I have recommended that you not worry about delivery, that we would solve any problems associated with it in force-breaking.

Now is the time to solve those problems, completely and finally. Here is where you learn how to force-break your youngster. After you have done so, you will be glad you did for the rest of his active life.

A dictionary definition of force-breaking might read like this:

> *A structured procedure by which a dog is trained to pick up, to hold, and to carry a dummy or bird on FETCH and to release it on GIVE.*

In the slow and gradual six-step process I describe, the youngster starts with a passive role, then moves into a somewhat more active role, and finally takes full responsibility for the job. Step One (accept, hold, and release) requires no force (as the term is used in this training). Nor does Step Two (carry). Force (mild discomfort to induce compliance) is first used in Step Three (reach) and continued in Step Four (pick up). During those steps, the dog goes through a necessary "period of resentment" as he learns this is "must" training, not "please." Step Five (jump) is an optional happy-em-up process, and Step Six transfers the skills learned in force-breaking to field work.

Many retriever trainers use an alternative technique, which is quick-and-rough. I call it "Hell Week," and do not recommend it to the amateur training his own dog.

WHY FORCE-BREAK?

You should force-break your retriever pup for several reasons.

First, you cannot get reliable delivery to hand without force-breaking. Any dog which has not been through this training will occasionally drop a bird. The force-broken dog will place the bird in your outstretched mitt every time.

Delivery to hand would not be such a big deal if the dog only dropped birds at the boss's feet. However, he can drop them other places, too, like at the edge of the water where the mud is soft and deep, leaving you the chore of slogging through gunk. Or he may leave it across a creek, or on the other side of a barbed-wire fence.

Picking up birds like these would be bad enough if they were all stone-dead, but they aren't. If your dog drops a lively cripple some distance away, you will probably not dine on that particular bird.

Look at it another way: Delivery to hand is a requirement in all formal retriever testing activities: AKC licensed field trials (all stakes), AKC hunting retriever tests (all stakes), UKC/HRC hunts (seasoned & finished stakes), and NAHRA hunting retriever tests (intermediate & senior stakes). If you plan to participate in any of these, you must force-break your retriever or risk blowing event after event due to delivery failures. The folks who know retriever work best—those who developed the rules for licensed field trials and hunting retriever tests—feel that delivery to hand is so important that they disqualify a dog that fails to do it even once in an entire trial, test, or hunt.

Delivery to hand facilitates the introduction of double marked retrieves. I tried starting Duffy out on doubles before he was force-broken, but he quickly showed me that I had made a mistake. A fast, stylish youngster with an insatiable desire to retrieve, he figured out his own way to do doubles: He raced out and picked up the first bird, flew back to within a few feet of me, and literally threw the bird to me—he had an amazingly accurate "arm"—and then took off after the other bird. Had I let this continue, I would have had a serious problem. He would have stopped to toss the bird farther and farther from me until he would have been running directly from one fall to the other, perhaps trying to bring in both at the same time. I didn't let it get that far. I force-broke him and then went back to doubles.

The second reason for force-breaking is to establish a framework for dealing with a couple of nasty problems that may come up in the dog's working life: hardmouth and stickiness.

A hardmouthed retriever is as worthless as a motorboat on the Mojave desert. If this fault isn't corrected quickly after it starts, it becomes incurable. The trouble is, it can get started so easily, even with dogs that have been extremely tender-mouthed for years. All it takes is one little accident.

For example, Misty, my Weimaraner of many years ago, was tender-mouthed almost to a fault. In the water she pushed the bird along with her open mouth until she landed, when she would, of course, take hold of it. One day she was returning a lightly hit pigeon in the water during training when the bird came to life and

We force-break retrievers . . . not to get them to retrieve, for they do that naturally . . . but to insure reliable delivery to hand, especially in water work. When coming out of water, the dog's natural inclination is to drop the bird and shake. That done, he may or may not pick the bird up again. The force-broken dog probably won't drop the bird, and will certainly pick it back up on command if he does.

tried to fly away. Before it got more than a few inches off the water, Misty lunged up and grabbed it, absolutely mangling it in the process. When she delivered it to me, it was mush. She had not intended to damage the bird. She only wanted to prevent it from getting away. However, she had flattened it about like an 18-wheeler would a tin can.

Had I done nothing, she would have soon had another accident—this one a little more deliberate—and another and another, until she became incurably hardmouthed.

To forestall that eventuality, I made Misty carry that mass of flesh, feathers, and bone chips for about 45 minutes out there in the July heat. She came to detest the bird quickly. I also didn't let her retrieve for thirty days, to allow her to forget the incident. She never flattened another bird, although she took a firmer grip on them in the water after that.

Had she not been force-broken, what could I have done? Nothing, because she would not have carried it on command that long. I would have had to stop and force-break her, then wait for the next "opportunity." All of the other supposed cures—nails through a bird, frozen birds, beating the dog with the bird, and so on—have one thing in common: They don't work.

"Stickiness" is different from hardmouth. A sticky retriever will not give up the bird on command—he "sticks" on it, refuses to release his grip. Most sticky dogs do not damage birds. They just won't surrender them. I have seen a person lift his sticky dog completely off the ground by raising the duck in its mouth. Like hardmouth, stickiness sets up quickly after it starts, so immediate measures are called for at the first indication of its onset.

What causes stickiness? It can be several things. For example, it is axiomatic that you should never punish a retriever while he still has a bird in his mouth, so trainers sometimes slip into the bad habit of taking a bird from a dog and immediately punishing him for some fault committed on the retrieve. It doesn't take a dog long to figure out that life is easier with the bird in its mouth than without it. Then, too, in the force-breaking process, some trainers praise for FETCH and not for GIVE. This encourages any tendency to stickiness the dog may have. Sometimes a dog will panic under excitement or pressure—especially at a field trial or hunting retriever test—and stick. There are probably other reasons, but these will give you some insight to the problem.

Whatever the cause, the cure is based on force-breaking, in which the dog is trained to release on the command GIVE. If a sticky dog has been force-broken, the cure can be administered immediately. If not, the cure will have to wait until the prerequisite force-breaking is completed.

Third, force-breaking enables you to solve some of the unusual problems that come up during hunting. For example, years ago I sent Misty after a crippled hen mallard that had fallen on a sandbar in the Arkansas River. When she neared the bird, it hissed and charged at her, chasing her back off the sandbar. Misty looked around at me as if to ask whether a duck could legitimately do that to a dog. I looked at her sternly and commanded FETCH! Misty then knew she had two choices: Tangle with the duck or with me. Since I was substantially the larger, she opted to battle it out with the bird. Landing like the Marines, she scooped up the still hissing Susie, and brought it back to me. I am sure that I would never have recovered that particular bird if Misty had not been force-broken. In fact, it is conceivable that she would have refused to pick up all crippled ducks afterwards if this one hen mallard had successfully bluffed her.

HISTORY OF FORCE-BREAKING

Force-breaking was first developed by a pointing breed trainer named David Sanborn back in the 1880s to teach basic retrieving to birddogs that lacked natural retrieving instinct, as many of them do.

Years ago I had a pointer, Jigger, that would hunt till he dropped, and point birds joyously all day, but would not retrieve. He might pick a shot bird up momentarily and give it a rough shake to make sure it was dead, but after that he would take off in search of new birds to point. His retrieving instinct was a big zero.

That is not uncommon among pointers and setters. Even those with some natural inclination to retrieve may lose it after a while. Birddog folks have recognized this for years, and have made appropriate adjustments. Some take spaniels or retrievers along; some pick up their own shot birds; still others insist that their birddogs do at least a minimal job of retrieving, so they force-break them.

David Sanborn developed the original force-breaking technique. Since his primary concern was training dogs to find and point birds, he developed his force-breaking technique so that it could be done in parallel with field work. That way he could run the dogs on birds in the morning and evening and force-break during the heat of the day. Further, he was in no hurry. If force-breaking took a month or more, who really cared?

Pointers and setters are typically high-strung and sensitive. Moreover, they must show "class" (animation, enjoyment) while working. Thus, Mr. Sanborn developed a force-breaking technique that was (and is) gentle, not damaging to the fragile psyches of his canine charges.

Trainers involved with the continental—or bobtailed—pointing breeds (German shorthairs, German wirehairs, Weimaraners, Vizslas, Brittanies, Griffons, and so on) are divided on force-breaking. Here too, it is used primarily to teach basic retrieving to dogs that just won't do it on their own. Since a high percent of the bobtails retrieve naturally, few owners have been compelled to rely on force-breaking. Even so, once a trainer has had to force-break his first one, he is apt to do it with all others thereafter because he is so pleased with the results.

Spaniel owners for the most part resist force-breaking. They argue that spaniels should retrieve naturally, not through force. However, since retrieving is such an important part of the spaniel's job, eventually these trainers will come to see some of the other advantages of force-breaking (delivery to hand, a framework for dealing with hard-mouth and stickiness). Retriever trainers were very slow to adopt force-breaking. James Lamb Free, in his 1949 classic, "Training Your Retriever," came out strongly against it. His argument was that a retriever should not have to be forced to do what he was bred to do.

Sometime between then and 1968, through that happy serendipity that seems to come to our assistance when we least expect it, retriever people discovered that force-breaking did a lot more than teach basic retrieving. The 1968 classic, "Charles Morgan on Retrievers," recommends force-breaking every retriever.

However, retriever pros have always faced a problem that bird-dog pros never had: They have to force-break very quickly. Let me explain. When an owner takes a dog to a pro, the pro knows that within a month that owner will be back to see how his dog is doing, and there had better be significant progress or the owner will probably take the dog back. That is a simple fact of life for all professional dog trainers, no matter what breeds they work with.

For the birddog trainer, that progress must be in finding and pointing birds. The owner won't care much about retrieving at first, as long as the dog is handling birds. Thus, the birddog trainer is under no pressure to get force-breaking over with in a hurry.

No so for the retriever pro. When the owner shows up at the end of the first month, the dog had better show significant progress in retrieving. The pro knows that progress beyond simple puppy stuff comes only after force-breaking has removed all the hassle about delivery. That means that he has about one week to force-break, so that he will have three weeks to work in the field before the owner returns. He cannot approach force-breaking slowly and gently like his birddog counterpart.

Therefore, the retriever pro invented Hell Week force-breaking. It is quick and very rough—on both dog and trainer. Every pro I have discussed this with hates it, but it is an economic fact of life for them. The problem is not any insensitivity on the part of the pros; it is the impatience of the owners.

Unfortunately, many amateur retriever trainers have adopted Hell Week, too, rather than the slower, more gentle techniques of the bird-dog trainers. Many of these amateurs don't really understand what they are doing; they are just mimicking the pros—in the one area most pros would change if they could. This is too bad, for the amateurs are not under the economic pressures that have led to Hell Week.

PREREQUISITES FOR FORCE-BREAKING

You can start force-breaking as soon as your dog is reliable on the following obedience commands: SIT, STAY, HEEL, COME-IN. Each of these is used in force-breaking.

However, force-breaking is demanding, so I prefer to wait until the pup convinces me he is a good prospect, that is, he likes birds, can mark satisfactorily, has style, wants to please, and is a dog I enjoy.

You should wash an unacceptable dog out early rather than wasting years of your life—which you don't get back—on him. I speak from too much of the opposite experience, for I have often spent a couple of years on a dog that I deep-down knew would never make the grade.

Pepper was a Lab female with one of the best pedigrees I have ever seen. However, she lacked consistency. She worked well about one day out of three. The rest of the time she showed too little interest in finding dummies and birds. Because of her excellent pedigree, I wasted over two years before I gave up on her.

I also wasted over two years on Mickey, a golden of my own breeding. He was a good dog, but not my kind. He was slow and methodical, whereas I like the snappy, fast retrievers. He was not too bright either, so I had to constantly devise new ways to get simple ideas across to him. I finally hardened my heart and placed him with a family of duck hunters. They loved him all his life, and still brag about what a great dog he was. To me he was just another wasted two years.

I force-broke both of these dogs, and didn't receive any benefit from my efforts. Such a waste. I hope you benefit from my mistakes and don't force-break a dog until you're reasonably sure he's a keeper.

Further, he should be at least seven months old, and nine months might even be better. However, I would not recommend waiting much past nine months because you should get force-breaking behind you early, so you can move on to more advanced field work, like multiple marks and blind retrieves.

EQUIPMENT

Besides the collar and lead you used in obedience training, you only need some sort of wooden force-breaking "buck" (an obedience trial dumbbell or dowel with legs). Later, of course, you will need retrieving dummies and birds.

As a "buck," I prefer a home-made affair because I can make it whatever size I want. I use 1.25" dowel for the cross-piece, and

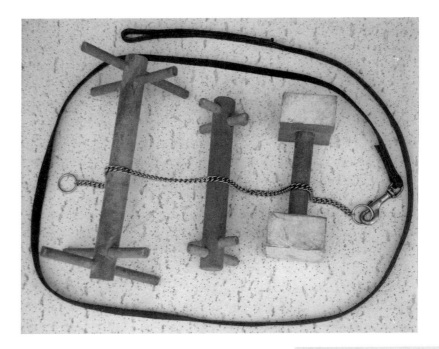

1/2" dowel for the legs. In the above photograph, the larger buck is 12" long with 3" legs. The smaller is 9" long with 1" legs. For years I used the larger size, but have recently changed to the smaller one, which is a bit handier.

However, if you don't want to make your own buck, you can do nicely with an obedience trial dumbbell of appropriate size. I have force-broken many dogs with them.

The legs (or solid block ends on the dumbbell) do two things. First, they hold the buck up off the ground when the dog

All the equipment you need for force-breaking: a six-foot lead, a chain training collar, and some sort of a "buck." Here three "bucks" are shown: a large home-made one, about 12" long with 3"legs; a small home-made one, about 9" long with 1" legs; and an obedience trial dumbbell, which is an adequate "buck substitute."

picks it up in Step Four. Second, they prevent him from allowing the buck to "accidentally" slip out of the side of his mouth as he holds it in Step One. If he wants to get rid of it, he has to spit it out.

YOUR ATTITUDE DURING FORCE-BREAKING

You should remember two things during this training: short sessions and plenty of praise.

Your sessions should not run over five minutes each. Many years ago I filmed the force-breaking of Tina, a Golden Retriever, using Super-8 sound film. Each 50-foot roll of film lasts three minutes and twenty seconds, and I was able to get each session on a single roll of film. If possible, do two or three sessions each day. However, if that is not possible, you can succeed with one session a day, although it will take you longer.

Praise speeds this training process. I have shown the film mentioned above to new retriever owners so often that my family has (understandably) long refused to watch it again, claiming it is devoid of plot and character, or something like that. They can no longer even stand the sound-track when they are in another part of the house. In fact, I can clear the house of all offspring by simply announcing that I am going to show the film to some new retriever trainers. It works even better than my old Glenn Miller records.

My kids call it the "Good Girl" movie because I say that so often during this 33-minute film. My wife tried to count the "Good Girl's" and gave up well past two hundred.

Yeah, all these "Good Girl's" are enough to drive my kids out of the house—but let me tell you, Tina never tired of them.

One other thing: Don't become discouraged. At some point with every dog I have ever force-broken, I have doubted whether I was making any progress. With some dogs, that has happened more than once. However, I have found that if I just persevere, every dog eventually comes around. You will surely hit this point with your dog, so be forewarned that it's coming, that it's normal, and that you can get past it if you just stick with the program.

RELATION TO FIELD WORK

In force-breaking, the dog goes through a "period of resentment" which, if transferred to field work, would cause him to refuse to retrieve, or "blink." To prevent your youngster from associating that resentment with field work, take the following precautions.

First, and perhaps most important, you should use an object for force-breaking that the pup will not connect with field work, like the buck described above. If you do the entire force-breaking job with it, your dog will never suspect that this training has anything to do with retrieving. Then, when the entire force-breaking process has been completed and the dog is over his resentment (in fact, has come to enjoy the work), you can introduce retrieving dummies and birds to transfer his new skills to regular field work without any risk of blinking.

Second, until force-breaking is complete, the commands, FETCH and GIVE, should never be used during field work. You may be tempted, once the dog is well started in force-breaking, to solve some little problem in the field with FETCH or GIVE. Don't do it, or your dog will make the connection you are working to avoid.

Third, do your force-breaking in the backyard, not in the field. Dogs are very "place conscious," and you shouldn't misuse this fact by force-breaking where you do your normal field training. You may get away with it, but why take the risk? Force-break in the backyard, the basement, or the garage.

Fourth, don't try to sweeten up the force-breaking process by using any field techniques. That too will cause the dog to make the connection before you are ready for him to do so.

A number of years ago I was helping a friend train his golden retriever. At the appropriate time I started him into force-breaking. It was a difficult process for the man, but he was making steady progress. We also continued the puppy field training in parallel.

One day something strange happened when my friend sent his golden for a retrieve in the field. The dog ran out, picked the dummy up, and started back, as usual. However, he dropped the dummy about half-way back and came on in without it. The dog had never done this before. I told my friend to rerun the test. This time the dog went out to the dummy but refused to pick it up; he returned without it. Clearly a blink.

I asked how force-breaking was going, because I suspected that was where the problem started. He told me it was going nicely, that he was almost through with the buck part. I asked him if he had had any problems in the past few days. He told me that the dog had

refused to pick the buck up off the ground, but that he had solved the problem by teasing him with the buck and tossing it a few feet. He said it worked like a charm. His dog had no further problem picking the buck up off the ground.

The trouble was that the dog made the connection between force-breaking and field work. My friend had used the buck exactly the way he had used the retrieving dummy when his dog was a small puppy—by teasing him with it and tossing it. His dog was not completely through his period of resentment, so he transferred his resentment to field work.

We had to stop all field work with that dog until force-breaking was completed, which fortunately was only a week or so in this case. However, it would have been so much better if this guy had worked through his force-breaking problem properly rather than improvising something based on play retrieving.

If you violate any of these simple rules and allow your dog to make the connection too soon, he will start blinking retrieves in the field. If that happens, you should discontinue field work immediately to prevent blinking from becoming a habit. A confirmed blinker is about as bad as a confirmed hardmouther. Either way you don't get your share of duck dinners.

Initially, to keep the buck in your dog's mouth, you will have to push his lower jaw up with your right hand, as the author does here with his young Golden, Deuce. Notice that the author has complete physical control because the lead is draped over his shoulder and anchored under his right foot. *Photo by Theresa Spencer.*

STEP ONE: ACCEPT AND HOLD THE BUCK

First, select a suitable place in which to work, a quiet place where your dog will not be distracted—the backyard, the basement, or maybe the garage. As I mentioned before, it should not be out in the field. Use this one place for all the initial force-breaking with the buck; when that is completed—before you introduce dummies and birds—you should go to different places, and sundry distractions, to convince your pup that FETCH and GIVE apply everywhere.

You must maintain physical control over your retriever during force-breaking. At times, especially during his period of resentment, he would gladly run off if he could. Different pros have worked out ingenious methods of maintaining physical control without restricting their own physical movement and comfort: an iron ring on the wall in a shed to which the dog is attached; a table with a stout cable overhead to which the dog is fastened; and so on. These are wonderful if you are force-breaking dogs regularly. However, the average amateur, who only force-breaks once every few years, can do nicely with nothing more than his chain training collar and a six-foot lead.

With your dog sitting at heel, wearing his chain collar with the lead attached, kneel beside him, throw the lead over your shoulder, and step on the end of it with your right foot. That gives you complete physical control without requiring the use of either hand. Further, the discomfort you gradually feel in this position reminds you to keep each session short.

Now, show the buck to your retriever. Let him smell it but not mouth it or play with it. You only want to prevent him from being intimidated by it, not make him think it is a new toy. In fact, the reaction you must achieve before proceeding is complete boredom. Then, he will resist your efforts as he should, allowing you opportunities to correct him.

Many beginners subconsciously want their dogs to go through force-breaking without any mistakes, and in less time than any other dog in history. I remember one man I tried to help with his first retriever. I explained force-breaking to him, showed him my movie, and told him it would probably take three to six weeks, perhaps longer, to do the job, but to hang in there and he would get it done. Two days later he called me and proudly announced that his dog was completely force-broken—all six steps, including dummies and birds.

I knew the dog wasn't yet well started in Step One, that he was never allowed to become bored with the buck, and that he had played through the steps without ever realizing that this is "must" training. There was no period of resentment, just a damned good time snatching that silly piece of wood from the boss's hand.

When I tried to explain that to the proud owner, he became very defensive. After all, he and his dog had just set a new record for speed in force-breaking, and he wasn't about to let me talk him out of such an accomplishment. Later, when it became obvious in field work that the dog was indeed not force-broken, this man found it easier to quit training than to admit that his "record" had never existed.

Be calm and deliberate. To succeed in force-breaking, you must establish a framework in which your dog resists and you insist. You must look on his resistance as a series of training opportunities. The dog which resists least is the most difficult to force-break, not the other way around.

Once your pup shows total boredom with the buck, open his mouth with your left hand, say FETCH, and insert the buck with your right. Put your right hand under his jaw to prevent him from spitting it out. Keep the buck in his mouth for a few seconds, all the time praising him quietly. Then, say GIVE and remove the buck. Again, praise him calmly.

Remember to praise on both FETCH and GIVE, but do it calmly, so your youngster remains serious about the business at hand.

Control his various efforts to avoid this training. If he turns away from the buck, bring his muzzle back around with your left hand. If he tries to spit it out, prevent it with your right hand under his chin. If he tries to get up and run off, jerk him back with the lead.

What should you do if the dog doesn't resist, but just sits there with the buck in his mouth? Wait him out. He will eventually tire of holding it and will try to drop it. Then, you say NO! and reinsert it with FETCH! Once resistance starts, you are making progress.

With resistance from the dog, the rest of Step One is fairly easy. Just repeat the FETCH-GIVE process several times each session. Gradually his resistance will decrease and he will start holding the buck voluntarily. Then, you should withdraw your right hand and wait a little longer before you say GIVE and take the buck. If he drops it, say NO! and reinsert the buck with a firm FETCH! Then, of course, praise him.

Years ago I had a problem with a golden named Tina at this point: She would not drop the buck when I removed my hand. Yes, that is a problem. I solved it by giving her a session near five mallard ducks I was keeping for training purposes. With that much distraction, she dropped the buck readily, so I was able to correct her and get her past this stage of training successfully.

When you have convinced your dog that he must hold the buck when your hand is not under his chin, try standing up (but keep your foot on the lead). If he drops the buck, correct him. Once he can handle that, leave him in a SIT-STAY with the buck in his mouth and step away from his side (but hold the end of the lead in your hand). Keep at this until you can walk to the end of the lead. Then, walk all the way around him.

The author heels Deuce while the youngster carries the buck. Deuce is heeling properly, but even if he weren't, the author wouldn't correct him for heeling errors . . . lest he knock the buck from the dog's mouth. Besides, the dog experiences enough corrections for dropping the buck, and so forth. He really doesn't need to be nagged about proper heeling, too. *Photo by Theresa Spencer.*

After he holds the buck through all this with no corrections, you might try introducing a few simple distractions, like clapping your hands or having a member of your family come into your training area unexpectedly. These should give you a few opportunities to teach the dog that he is not allowed to drop the buck until you say GIVE, no matter what.

STEP TWO: CARRY THE BUCK

Once your retriever holds the buck reliably while you walk around him, you can move on to Step Two. Here you teach him to carry the buck, first at heel and then when you call him to you.

Start by having him hold the buck as you kneel, as in Step One. Then, stand up, command HEEL, and start walking. He will probably spit it out before taking his first step. Wonderful, for that gives you a chance to correct him. If he hangs on and heels properly, continue walking and praising until he does drop it, which probably won't take long. As you walk, praise him as long as he holds the dummy. As soon as he drops it, say NO!, stop, reinsert the buck into his mouth with FETCH! and then continue heeling and praising.

He will gradually realize that he not only can but also must walk and carry the buck at the same time. There are two cautions

here: Be careful that you don't bump the buck out of his mouth while heeling; and don't be too picky about how well he heels.

If you bump the buck from his mouth, correct him gently as you replace it. Were he to get off with no correction, he might start deliberately bumping the buck against your leg just to get away with dropping it. Dogs can be crafty.

If he heels sloppily, don't correct him too often or too enthusiastically, for you may cause him to drop the buck. Should that happen, correct him gently and continue.

After he heels reliably while carrying the buck, have him carry it when you call him to you. Leave him in a SIT-STAY, walk to the end of the lead (you must maintain physical control), and call him to you. If he drops the buck, rush at him and make the usual correction. However, if you have completed the heeling work as you should have, he will probably carry it all the way the first time.

After he has shown you that he can carry the buck while coming to you on the six-foot lead, you can lengthen it out a little. Let him drag the lead at first, but after he has demonstrated his reliability, you can take him off-lead and call him from across the backyard.

In each session, have him heel with the buck for a while, and call him to you two or three times.

Also, in each session, continue the Step One work: FETCH, GIVE, FETCH, GIVE, FETCH, GIVE. By the time he is carrying reliably, he should frequently open his own mouth during these Step One drills.

Once again, I should mention the importance of praise. Whenever you are not correcting him, you should be praising him. You are giving him some pretty tough "must" training. Knowing when he is pleasing you, as well as when he is not, speeds the training. It also maintains a positive attitude for both of you.

STEP THREE: OPENING AND REACHING

Throughout Step Two, you have opened your dog's mouth and inserted the buck. His role has been passive: holding, carrying, and releasing on command. Now, in Step Three you teach your retriever to take a more active part in the process. First, he must open his own mouth when you say FETCH. Then he will have to reach for the buck.

To teach him these new accomplishments you must apply "force"—a certain amount of pain—whenever he fails to comply. You have four types of force from which to choose: the lip pinch, the ear pinch, the paw squeeze, and the choke.

The Lip Pinch: You grasp the dog's muzzle and press his lip against his canine tooth hard enough to induce pain as you open his mouth.

There are several advantages to this method. It is a natural extension of the previous training. You can adjust the pain level to the needs of the individual dog easily. It gives you absolute control over the dog's head and muzzle.

There is one disadvantage: Your hand blocks the dog's view of the buck. This is not serious, but it is a disadvantage relative to the other methods of force.

The lip pinch is my personal favorite. I have used it successfully for a lot of years with a lot of dogs.

The Ear Pinch: You pinch the little flap on the back of the dog's ear, and as the dog cries out, he open his mouth. Some trainers pinch the ear flap against the ring on the collar for greater effect.

The advantages of the ear pinch are that it allows the dog to have good visibility of the buck and that it takes little strength to create enough pain to get the attention of the hardest-headed dog on earth.

The disadvantages are that it gives poor control over the dog's muzzle, and that it doesn't allow you to adjust the pain level to the individual needs of the dog. After a number of pinches, it hurts a lot no matter how lightly the pinch is applied.

The standard for retriever pros who use Hell Week, its effectiveness depends on the ear being sensitized by a lot of pinches in a short period of time. In the more gentle force-breaking technique that I recommend, you may not have to apply force frequently enough for the ear pinch to become effective.

I once met an elderly gentleman with one hand missing who always used the ear pinch to force-break his dogs. He had a mental pincher device attached to his arm in place of his hand, and he could deliver a fearsome pinch with it.

The Paw Squeeze: You squeeze one of the dog's front paws. That will open any canine mouth that hasn't been wired shut, believe me!

The advantages are that the dog has good visibility of the buck and you can easily adjust the pain level to the needs of the individual dog.

The disadvantages are that it gives almost no control over the dog's muzzle, and it is difficult to apply in the field if the dog has a mental lapse after force-breaking is completed.

Deuce reaches for the buck, which the author holds very near the ground. Getting to this point took several sessions, of course, but Deuce was a most cooperative "student," as his enthusiasm in this picture shows. *Photo by Theresa Spencer.*

This is the traditional David Sanborn method of force, used by birddog trainers almost exclusively for over 100 years. Some pros use a variation called the "nerve hitch," in which a cord is wrapped around the dog's toes and jerked sharply. Personally, I feel that this may help the pro who has to force-break dogs day in and day out, but is of little use to the occasional force-breaker.

The Choke: You position the chain training collar high on the dog's neck, right behind the ears, and jerk the lead up sharply, which will definitely open his mouth.

The major advantage of this method is that it gives the dog good visibility of the buck as force is being applied.

The disadvantages are that it doesn't give good control over the dog's muzzle, and it is difficult to adjust the amount of force to the individual requirements of each dog.

Nevertheless, there are many trainers with outstanding credentials who use this method.

Take your pick. In the following text I say "apply force," and leave the kind of force up to you.

If you have waited to start Step Three until your dog frequently opens his own mouth, you should get through this step faster and easier. Once, when I rushed things with a female Labrador that wasn't too bright, I found myself applying force more often and more intensely than usual, and it really bothered me. I went back to Step

One and conditioned her more thoroughly. Instead of just grasping her muzzle and opening her mouth as I said FETCH, I inserted my fingers into her mouth and pried her lower jaw downward, as she would do in opening her own mouth. After a few sessions, her lower jaw began to drop automatically when I said FETCH. Then, I was able to advance to Step Three without using what I considered too much force.

The dog will resent the work in this step much more than he has that in Steps One and Two. This is where the "period of resentment" begins. However, with the build-up of Steps One and Two, this resentment should not be intense or long-lasting.

Start out kneeling beside your sitting dog. Physical control is more important than ever, so toss the lead over your shoulders and secure the end of it under your right foot.

Place the buck directly in front of the dog's muzzle, almost touching it, and say FETCH. If he opened his own mouth, fine; insert the buck and praise the dog as usual. If he doesn't open, apply force and insert the buck—THEN PRAISE LAVISHLY. Praise him every time he does things right, no matter how much force you had to apply. He will come along much faster if he never has any doubt about when he is pleasing you.

Repeat this over and over through several sessions, until he always opens automatically on FETCH. Do not expect him to reach for the buck until he is absolutely reliable at opening voluntarily. Rushing things only makes the entire process more difficult for both of you, and may slow it down, too.

When you can get through an entire five-minute session without force, teach him to reach. Try this little shortcut: Heel your dog around without the buck; then put it in front of his mouth—continue moving as you do—and say FETCH. Since he opens automatically, his own motion will cause him to reach for it. Do this several times until he is comfortable with this new exercise. Naturally, apply force anytime he refuses to open, which should not happen often now.

With that background in reaching while heeling, try it with him sitting beside you. Place the buck an inch or so in front of his mouth and say FETCH. He will probably open but not reach. Fine, just

Deuce goes out, picks up the buck, and returns to heel. This is a big step for most dogs. Before this step, he has always taken the buck from the trainer's hand, but now it lies by itself on the ground. For some reason, this baffles many dogs at first. *Photo by Theresa Spencer.*

push his head forward with your left hand so that his mouth goes around the buck. Continue this until he reaches before you push his head forward. Intersperse this drill with plenty of reaching while heeling, and it should not take long until he will reach an inch or two on his own. Naturally, apply force anytime he refuses to open.

After he is reaching with reasonable regularity—enough so that you know he understands what you expect of him—apply force anytime he refuses to reach (even though he may have opened voluntarily).

Then, gradually lengthen the distance he must reach. Lengthen down below his mouth, off to either side, and *slightly* above his head. Do not position the buck where he would have to get up to reach it yet. That comes later. However, it shouldn't take long to get him to reach almost to the ground in front of him to take it. Anytime he refuses, apply force and make him comply.

He will undoubtedly try a new ploy: looking away from the buck. If you hold the buck on the left side of his head, for example, he will look to his right. He is trying to con you into believing that he can't see the buck and therefore shouldn't be expected to reach for it. To convince him otherwise, hold the buck in place, and say FETCH. If he refuses, apply force and make him go to the buck. He must learn that it is his responsibility to go to the buck when you say FETCH; it is not your responsibility to move the buck to where it is convenient for him.

After he learns the joy of avoiding force by acting quickly, he may not wait for you to say FETCH. He may open and reach as soon as he sees the buck. While that indicates that he is hearing the gospel you are preaching, you shouldn't allow it. Say NO and restrain him. He must open and reach only on the command FETCH, not when-ever he sees the buck.

When he reaches for and takes the buck when it is held almost on the floor in front of him—reliably, which means almost every time—he is ready to move on to Step Four.

Throughout Step Three, continue the Step Two training, that is, have your retriever carry the buck at heel and while being called to you. Do this every session.

STEP FOUR: PICKING UP

Next, you train your youngster to pick the buck up off the ground. Although this is a natural extension of the reaching in Step Three, many dogs balk here. Until now, you have held the buck in your hand every time you commanded FETCH. Now, you lay it down first. This subtle difference confuses many dogs.

Misty, the first dog I ever force-broke, balked for a month. If I held the buck on the ground, she picked it up. If I took my hand off of it, she refused. Since I was inexperienced, and overly soft with her, I wasted too much time working her through this problem. Today, I would apply more force and solve it in two or three days at the most.

To ease your pup into picking up the buck off the ground, start it while heeling. Heel your dog and periodically have him reach for the buck as he walks, just as you did in Step Three. Then, "accidentally" drop it as you say FETCH. He may pick it up before he realizes that something is different. Of course, if he refuses, apply force. However, if you handle this deftly, he will probably not refuse.

After he has done this several times, ease him into picking it up while sitting at heel. Start out by having him reach a few inches straight in front of him. Then hold the buck farther and farther away until he has to stand up and move forward to get it, even though you are still holding it off the floor. Have him return to heel with it. When he moves away and back to heel comfortably, place the buck on the floor far enough in front of him so that he has to get up to pick it up. Because of the preparatory work you have done, he should move out, pick it up, and return to heel. If he refuses, apply force, and repeat the pick-up while heeling.

The very essence of force-breaking is picking up and returning to heel. Whenever your dog accidentally drops a bird, a simple FETCH should induce him to pick it up and deliver to your hand. In hunting, in field trialing, and in hunting tests, you need that response. Consequently, you should drill on this a lot once he has mastered it. Place the buck directly in front of him a few feet, then off to each side, then behind him. Of course, praise every success as well as correct every failure.

STEP FIVE: JUMPING

Once your dog consistently gets up, goes out a few feet, picks the buck up off the floor, and returns to heel with it, his resentment rapidly disappears. In fact, he should show signs of genuinely enjoying his new skill.

Step Five is pure fun-and-games, intended to sweeten him up and remove the last trace of resentment from his attitude. You have taught him that he absolutely *must* obey the commands FETCH and GIVE. You have led him through a very necessary period of resentment to reinforce those commands. Now, you should lighten things up a bit and help him come to enjoy FETCH and GIVE.

To remove the last traces of resentment without losing the control you have established, you teach your retriever to jump up for the

buck. Dogs really enjoy this, once they find out they can handle it.

Start out while heeling. As you move along, hold the buck a few inches above the dog's head and command FETCH. He will raise up off his front legs to reach for it. Great. Praise him lavishly, even excitedly here, for you want to pump him up a bit. Do this several times each session until he is actually leaving the ground to jump for the buck.

Next, try it while the dog is sitting at heel. Shorten up, too, to just a few inches above his head. Let him learn gradually that he can succeed at this new aspect of the game. Eventually, he will jump as high as you want from a sitting position when you hold the buck over his head and command FETCH. Personally, I never hold it higher than my shoulders (and I am quite short), for I am more interested in sweetening the dog up with easy jumps than I am in setting a new height record. I have seen men who are quite tall hold the buck over their heads. This is showboating, not training. Stick to shoulder height.

After working your dog through his slight and short-lived period of resentment during Step Four, "sweeten him up" with some jumping in Step Five. This eliminates the last trace of resentment, for most dogs really enjoy jumping up for the buck . . . as Deuce demonstrates here. *Photo by Theresa Spencer.*

Once your dog will jump a reasonable height for the buck, your force-breaking with the buck is completed. You used the buck to channel your dog's resentment away from dummies and birds and to thereby allow you to continue field work during the force-breaking process. Now you no longer need the buck as a decoy. You are now ready for Step Six, in which you will transfer force-breaking to dummies and birds so you can use it in actual field work.

A few dogs do not take to this jumping routine. My Chesapeake, Beaver, is one of those. He disdained it, indicating by his attitude that I wasn't fooling him one bit. He would FETCH and GIVE, but he wouldn't play silly games for me. I didn't push it any further. After all, this is supposed to happy the dog up, not start a new kind of resentment.

In Step Six, you transfer this training to dummies and birds . . . and begin using commands FETCH and GIVE in the field. Here Deuce picks up a dummy and is about to return to heel with it. He seems to be saying, "Hey, if you'd told me this is where we were heading, I would've been much more cooperative!" *Photo by Theresa Spencer.*

STEP SIX: DUMMIES AND BIRDS

You can now transfer force-breaking to the various dummies and birds you use in the field. However, there are a few precautions you should observe to avoid getting into a battle of wills with your dog.

1. Don't introduce any dummy or bird that your dog has not previously retrieved. You are extending FETCH and GIVE to retrieving objects with which your dog is already familiar—not advancing his work to things he has never handled before.

You have continued puppy field work while force-breaking, so he should be acquainted with two or three different types of dummies, as well as pigeons, pheasants, and ducks. If not, delay Step Six of force-breaking until he has come to love all of these in field work.

The Lab Katie was small, so I used only small plastic dummies in her field work. Forgetting that when I force-broke her, I hit a stone wall of refusals when I tried to get her to handle the large dummies on FETCH. I had to back up and have her retrieve them in the field for some time before she would accept them on FETCH.

2. Increase the size of the dummies and birds gradually. Start out with the small plastic and canvas dummies, then bring in the large plastic and canvas dummies. Next, use dead pigeons. Then, take him through the routine with a small dead duck. A teal is ideal if you have one; if not, a hen mallard will do. After that, try a dead drake mallard. You can intersperse dead pheasants into the process during the large duck routine.

3. With each new object, start in Step One and go through Step Five. Let your dog become comfortable with it before proceeding. Then, open his mouth, say FETCH and insert the dummy or bird—and be ready to prevent him from dropping it with your right hand under his chin. When he will sit and hold it without attempting to spit it out, start Step Two (carrying); when he can handle that, go on to Step Three (opening and reaching), and so on. Don't rush him on any dummy or bird. Go through all the steps.

4. Remember to praise success lavishly as you go through each step with each new dummy and bird.

Once you have introduced all these dummies and birds into the force-breaking routine with your dog, you should begin using FETCH and GIVE in the field. If he drops a bird or dummy, make him pick it up with FETCH. If you think he is about to drop one, say FETCH to make him hold it. Anytime he refuses to comply with FETCH or GIVE—which should be damned seldom—apply force convincingly.

HEY, YOU MADE IT!

You have now joined a rather elite group of trainers: those who have successfully force-broken a retriever. You are a real dog trainer now, and nothing in the rest of the retriever training process should worry you. You can handle it. You have proved that by handling the most difficult part: force-breaking.

If you are proud of your dog, you should be. If you are even more proud of yourself, you should be. Congratulations.

GUN

BIRD

DOG   HANDLER

DOUBLE MARKED RETRIEVES

THE NATURE OF DOUBLES

Every hunter, even the occasional one who shoots as poorly as I do, now and again knocks down two birds from a single flock or flush. Therefore, every retriever that does solid work on singles should be extended to doubles. Besides, the training demands more teamwork, more involvement of the handler, so it is as enjoyable as it is practical.

In a double, two birds are thrown and shot, one at a time, in different areas. The retriever must watch ("mark") each "fall" in turn, and then retrieve them one at a time. This means that he must remember the one he retrieves last all the time he is retrieving the first one. A double tests not only his marking ability but also his memory.

The retriever naturally picks up the second bird down first, and the first bird down second. Thus, the first bird down is called the "memory bird," because it is the one the dog must remember longer. The second bird down is called the "diversion," because it diverts the dog's attention from the other bird.

A double is many times more difficult than a single. The possible variations in throwing sequences and directions increase almost geometrically. In a single, there are no sequence variations, and each throw must go either left or right. In a double either fall may be first, and each may be thrown left or right. Thus there are four possible combinations of direction: both left, both right, both out, both in.

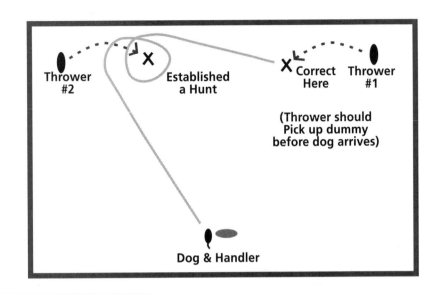

Thrower #2

Established a Hunt

X Correct Here   Thrower #1

(Thrower should Pick up dummy before dog arrives)

Dog & Handler

FIG. 6: A switch and where to correct the dog
Here the dog switched from the diversion bird to the memory bird. He went to the diversion bird area, established a hunt, then left that area to go to the memory bird area. In correcting the switch, to take advantage of the canine "place consciousness" relative to punishment, you should wait until he reaches the area to which he switches before correcting him. Of course, have the thrower pick up the bird (or dummy), so your dog won't get it before you can correct him.

Then, too, the falls may be the same distance from the line or either may be farther than the other.

Doubles also introduce a very challenging problem that doesn't exist in singles: switching.

SWITCHING

A retriever switches when he gives up on one bird and tries to retrieve the other. He can do this in three ways. First, he may pick up the diversion bird, then drop it to go after the memory bird. Second, he may hunt for the diversion bird, fail to find it, and leave to hunt for the memory bird. Third, he may hunt for the memory bird, fail to find it, and return to the area of the diversion bird. Some purists argue that this last is not a "true" switch, since there is no longer a bird in the area to which the dog switched. However, it is the same mental error, and the correction in training is the same, so I consider it a switch.

In each type of switch, the dog demonstrates a lack of persistence. He gives up on one bird and tries to retrieve the other. Obviously, a dog cannot give up until after he has "established a hunt." If a dog starts toward one bird, but half-way there changes his mind and goes to the other bird, he has not technically switched. This often happens when a handler tries to "select" (pick up the memory bird first) with an inexperienced dog. Sometimes, even when the handler doesn't select, some wild notion arises in the dog's mind. I have occasionally seen a dog run straight through the area of the diversion bird without establishing a hunt, then go to the area of the memory bird to make his first retrieve. No hunt in the diversion bird area, so no lack of persistence, so no switch. In these situations the dog demonstrates some degree of confusion, and will be less likely to complete both retrieves successfully, but he hasn't switched.

Why does switching deserve all these hair-splitting examples? Because it is a very serious fault, in and of itself adequate reason for disqualification in field trials, hunting tests, and working certificate tests. Those who know retriever work best—the people who wrote the rules for all these formal activities—consider switching that serious a problem.

Why do they find it so objectionable? There are several reasons. First, it shows a lack of persistence, which is a serious fault in any hunting dog. Second, a dog that switches disturbs a lot of cover unnecessarily between the areas of the falls. If there are birds there, the switching dog may flush them out of range. Finally, a switching dog normally does not successfully complete the double. Frequently, he doesn't retrieve either bird because he grows more and more confused, switches back and forth, and eventually forgets both marks.

A dependable retriever should stick with each retrieve, diligently hunting a reasonable area around the fall until he finds the bird. However, this trait is more trained than natural. Every retriever will switch under conditions of sufficient temptation until trained not to. So "switch-proofing" is a major part of the double marked retrieve training program.

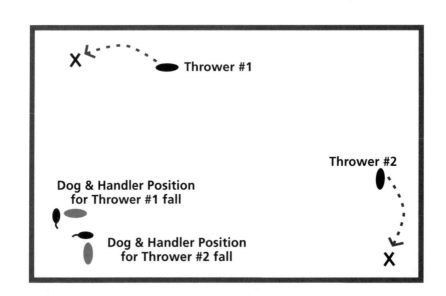

Thrower #1

Thrower #2

Dog & Handler Position
for Thrower #1 fall

Dog & Handler Position
for Thrower #2 fall

X

**FIG. 7: Positioning the dog
for each fall**
In a double mark, start out
facing the memory bird
(#1). After it is down, turn
to face the diversion bird
(#2). By doing this, you
give your dog the best possible look at both falls . . .
and you position him to
retrieve the diversion bird
first, which is the natural
sequence for dogs.

PREREQUISITES

To be ready for doubles, your young retriever should be doing good work on singles, be
steady, and be force-broken.

Good work on singles: If he cannot
pick up reasonably difficult singles out to
about 100 yards in various conditions of
cover, terrain, and wind, you would only
confuse him with doubles. However, if you
have the time, you could begin bare-ground
doubles in parallel with singles in cover.

Steady: The breaking retriever doesn't
stick around long enough to see both falls.
Just as a baseball batter can't hit 'em if he
can't see 'em, so a retriever won't find 'em if he doesn't mark 'em.
You should continue using the belt cord as you teach doubles. Many
retrievers that are rock-steady on singles try to break on doubles at
first. A retriever learns steadiness in pieces: first on singles, then on
doubles, then on triples, and so on.

Force-broken: In teaching doubles, you should do everything
you can to help your pup remember the second fall. Any hassle at the

line as he delivers the first bird dims his memory of the other one. The non-force-broken retriever may drop the first bird anywhere in the vicinity of the line and return to you without it. That forces you to delay sending him for the second retrieve long enough to pick up the dropped bird. If you don't, your young retriever will probably return to it when you send him after the other fall.

THE HANDLER'S RESPONSIBILITIES

Your job is to help your retriever do his job. He is responsible for marking and retrieving two birds now, but you can assist him in several inconspicuous ways.

In a double mark, as your dog returns with the diversion bird, turn to face the memory bird. That way when he sits to deliver, he will be facing the next retrieve. Here Mike Gallagher turns to face the memory bird thrower (wife Mary Jo) as his Flat-Coat, Scandal (Harmony's Black Sox Scandal SH WCX UDX, HoF), returns with the diversion bird (here a dummy).

First, even if you have been sitting in a blind and pointing a gun in your singles, go back to the KISS approach to handling. Start every test standing up with your dog sitting at heel. Your throwers should be in plain sight again, too. After your retriever can handle

Right: After your dog has delivered the diversion bird, hold it behind your hip on the side opposite the dog. There it's out of sight and out of mind for the dog. Here Mary Jo Gallagher demonstrates with her Flat-Coat, Fortune.

Left: As the handler, you are responsible for knowing when to send your dog for each retrieve. To do this, you should watch your dog, not the throwers. Here Mike Gallagher is watching as his Flat-Coat, Scandal, looks the wrong way. Mike will encourage Scandal to look towards the fall (straight ahead) before sending him.

Here Scandal is properly locked in on the fall, so Mike Gallagher prepares to send him. Only by watching the dog can the handler know when to . . . and when not to . . . send his dog.

tough doubles in cover and in water, and has been switch-proofed, you can add the refinements you need for hunting and hunting tests: stools, duckblinds, pointing the shotgun, hidden throwers.

Next, you should respect your youngster's desire to retrieve doubles in the natural sequence (or Biblical sequence: "The last shall be first and the first shall be last").

In the more advanced stakes at field trials and hunting tests, experienced handlers sometimes "select" retrieves out of the natural sequence. However, they do that with older, more experienced dogs.

That doesn't work so well in stakes for younger dogs. In a derby stake I judged some years ago, I stood sadly by and watched an inexperienced handler "select" his young Lab out of first and into third place in the final water double. The pup overruled him and retrieved in the natural sequence, but was so bothered and confused by the boss's handling that he was wobbly on both birds. Actually, that handler was lucky to take third place, since many young dogs would have bombed out under such circumstances.

You should make sure your pup locates both throwers before you call for the birds. True, you can't do that in hunting or in hunting tests. However, right now you are just introducing him to doubles, so help him all you can. However, don't stand at the line and point out each thrower. That too often becomes a bad habit that is difficult to break. Simply heel your dog to the line along a path that allows him to locate them on his own.

You can use your own body movements at the line to help your youngster. Start off facing the memory bird thrower. After that bird is down, turn to face the diversion bird thrower, using the belt cord to encourage your dog to shift around with you. After awhile, he will shift with you automatically, and you can later transfer that to the direction in which you point your shotgun.

As your pup returns to you with the diversion bird, rotate around to face the memory bird. That way, when he sits to deliver, he faces his next retrieve. Then, you only need to take the bird, let him lock in, and send him. No hassle between birds.

You should handle the delivered diversion bird so that it doesn't distract your dog. The technique is simple: Reach around with your right hand and take whichever end of the bird is nearer to you; then, hold the bird behind your right hip before sending the dog again. That way, you get the retrieved bird out of sight and out of the dog's mind. If you take it with your left hand and hold it near the dog, the bird distracts the dog when he should be concentrating on the memory bird. I have seen dogs waste time and lose concentration by repeatedly jumping up after a bird thusly held.

You must also know how to send your retriever for each mark. First off, you should look at your dog, not at the fall. If you look at the fall, you don't know whether your dog is properly locked in or swinging his head away. If you send him when he is looking the wrong way, he will wander off like a drunken sailor and never complete the retrieve.

Should you use your left hand to give a line to the fall? The diversion bird is fresh in your dog's mind, so why distract him that way? Simply give him the command to retrieve. Ditto for the memory bird if he locks in on it and seems confident that he knows where it is. If not, your hand can help him recall it. Even then, don't use a bowler's arm sweep. Don't even flick your fingers. Just place your hand alongside his head, let him lock in, and send him. This slight use of your hand can help him remember his mark, but doesn't distract him after he locks in.

EQUIPMENT

You need no additional types of equipment for doubles. However, you need more dummies, and you need two blank pistols. Ideally, each member of your training group has his own pistol and dummies. If you use all of your dummies communally, write your name on yours in indelible ink to facilitate sorting them out at the end of each training session.

BARE GROUND WORK

Because doubles are so much more difficult than singles, you should go back to bare ground to introduce them. If you start out in cover, your retriever will make so many mistakes initially—breaking, forgetting the memory bird, switching—that both of you will become discouraged. You will also take longer to complete the training.

You should set up the initial bare ground doubles so that your dog can easily find both dummies and cannot switch. That way he learns to do it right and he receives plenty of praise, no corrections. To make sure he finds both dummies, use highly visible big white ones. To prevent him from switching, do these initial doubles with a barrier (fence, building, even a row of cars) between the falls.

When I started doubles with my Chesapeake-in-residence, Beaver, I tossed them down the two sides of my kennel runs. That kept him from switching the normal way. However, it didn't dissuade him from trying to run right through me to get to the other dummy. I had to play line-backer to his full-back, and tackle him. Beaver is 90 pounds of muscle, and he was going full-throttle every time. More often than not, we rolled in the grass after I tackled him. Sometimes he dragged me a few feet before I gained control. I hope you have an easier time of it.

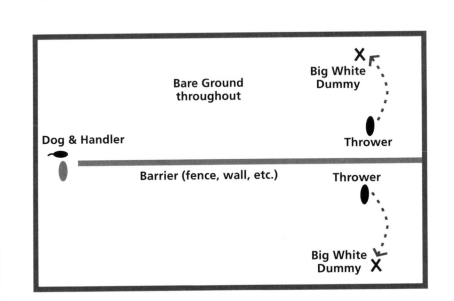

Bare Ground throughout

Big White Dummy **X**

Dog & Handler

Thrower

Barrier (fence, wall, etc.)

Thrower

Big White Dummy **X**

FIG. 8: Initial doubles with barrier
In your dog's initial double marks on bare ground, prevent switching by having the dummies thrown on opposite sides of a barrier (fence, wall, whatever). That way, he learns to retrieve doubles one at a time without correction, and he develops confidence, too.

A tennis court fence does nicely. Stand at the corner and toss one fall down each side. Later, when your dog understands that he is to retrieve them one at a time, you can go onto the tennis court itself and use the net as the barrier. The net isn't as impenetrable as the outside fence, but it still discourages switching. Another good barrier is one of those old-time schoolyard fences, made of eight or ten-foot high chain link with frequent openings for traffic. You can set the line up at any of the openings and toss one fall on either side of the fence. You can also start at the corner of a barn or large building.

Initially you can toss both dummies yourself, but you should recruit a couple of assistants as soon as possible. You need to be free to concentrate on handling the dog while others do the throwing.

Have the throwers vary the sequence and direction frequently: left-right; right-left; both throwers near the fence, throwing away from it; both standing out some distance, throwing towards it; one out, one in; and so on. Have them also vary their distances from the line: both the same distance; one farther away than the other. If your dog becomes accustomed to these variations in his bare ground, he will cope with them more easily when you move in cover.

Practice all your handling techniques while working with the barrier. Bring your dog to the line at heel along a path that allows him to locate both guns before arriving at the line. Sit him at heel facing the memory bird thrower. Do not use STAY to steady him. Shift to face the diversion bird thrower after the memory bird is down. Send your dog without any hand waving, just the command to retrieve. As he returns to you with the diversion bird, turn and face the memory bird. When he sits at heel to deliver, take the dummy with your right hand and hide it behind your right hip. Allow the dog time to relocate the memory bird—which should be easy, since you are using big white dummies at first—and then send him to retrieve it.

Here on bare ground, with a barrier and big white dummies, your dog cannot fail, no matter how poorly you handle him. Later, your handling will make his job easier or more difficult, so practice doing things the right way here when mistakes don't matter much.

Stay with the barrier until your dog is comfortable with doubles and you have so drilled proper handling techniques into your subconscious that you no longer have to think about them. Then, move away from the barrier for more advanced bare ground work.

The initial doubles without a barrier should be very widespread, at least 120 degrees apart. You are still conditioning your dog to do them correctly, not tempting him to switch. Later, when he truly understands his role in doubles, you will make switching more appealing to afford yourself opportunities to convince him that it is a bad idea. But not yet.

Continue to drill him on all the throwing sequence and direction variations. Also, lengthen him out to about 100 to 120 yards for each fall. Initially use nothing but big white dummies for greater visibility. You want to build confidence, based on success, success, success.

As a general rule, set up all your tests downwind. A crosswind is OK, as long as it does not blow scent from the memory bird to the dog as he goes to retrieve the diversion. If it does that, it will encourage him to switch, obviously, and in correcting him for the switch, you will be telling him to ignore his nose—which "ain't too bright" for a trainer. Avoid retrieves into the wind—either directly or quartering—for this will encourage the dog to quarter (zig-zag) to the falls rather than run straight lines. Later, after he is fully trained and conditioned to run straight lines to his marks, an occasional retrieve directly into the wind won't do any harm. However, such retrieves will set up the wrong habits in the young dog.

In all of this, you must be intelligent enough to understand that training is not hunting, training is not hunting tests, training is training, period. You train to help your dog establish the right habits. Once that is done, you can use exotic tests in the polishing process. We don't teach calculus in the early grades, before the students are familiar with the basics, do we?

When your dog is doing well out to 100 yards with the falls 120 degrees apart, start rerunning every test with dark dummies. If he has a problem with the memory bird, back up and use a dark dummy for the diversion and a white one for the memory bird for a while. If that causes him no problems—and it shouldn't because the memory bird is visible from the line—then rerun with both dark dummies.

Then, start using dark dummies on the first run of each test. Still keep the 120 degree angle between the falls. He isn't ready for switching tests yet. Vary the length of the falls frequently, rather than always operating at his maximum distance. You would be surprised how poorly a dog does on short retrieves if he doesn't get them very often.

While he is readily handling dark dummies on the first run of tests with the angle of 120 degrees at all distances out to about 100 yards, you should shorten up, go back to white dummies, and reduce the angle between the falls. You do this to tempt him to switch, so you can correct him and convince him that switching is a bad idea. Reduce the angle to 90 degrees, and then to 60, but nothing less than that. The dog must clearly understand which dummy he is being sent for before he can be corrected for switching.

Have the falls thrown "both in," that is, toward each other, for this maximizes the temptation to switch. Make sure, however, that the dummies fall where they are 60 degrees apart. The throwers should be at a greater angle, obviously.

Your dog may not attempt to switch in any of this bare ground work. If he doesn't, that is OK. Don't press him by reducing the angle to less than 60 degrees. You might try using a dark diversion dummy and a white memory bird dummy. If that doesn't induce him to switch, let it go and do your initial switch-proofing in cover.

However, if he does try to switch, there are two things to remember: He must not succeed, which means that the thrower must pick up the dummy before the dog gets to it; and you must correct the animal in the area to which he switches—to take advantage of his "place-consciousness" relative to punishment. A dog avoids a place in which he has been punished.

Say nothing as your dog switches. Instead, run out there, catch him, and punish him in the area to which he switched. If he has left that area, run him down and drag him back. Don't call him to you. Don't stop him with the whistle. Don't heel him back.

How severely you correct him depends on his temperament, but he will quickly tell you how much is too much, as I will soon explain.

After correcting him in the area to which he switched, heel him to the dummy he should have retrieved. Tell him to FETCH, then to SIT and STAY. Walk back to the line and call him in. Then praise him! He has done it right, even though you helped him plenty, so praise him.

Then, rerun the entire test. If he switches again, you didn't correct him vigorously enough. If he refuses to return to the area in which you corrected him to make a normal retrieve, you overdid it. If he does the test properly, you corrected him about right. This is one of the few places in retriever training in which the dog tells you almost immediately whether your correction was proper or not.

That is the basic correction for switching. You should use it from now on, whenever your retriever affords you the opportunity. Switch-proofing takes time. Even after you have him well into triples, he may occasionally switch. However, if you consistently correct him as I described above, you will succeed in time.

COVER

Naturally, you should make the initial doubles in cover very short and very wide; thirty yards long with 120 degrees between the falls. Keep the hazards simple, too. Reasonably level terrain, light to moderate cover, downwind falls. Trial and success in the beginning gives the dog a good attitude towards each new phase of his training.

You should use the following three techniques to insure success: salting, rehearsing, and rerunning.

"Salting" has already been discussed in the chapter on single marks. A temporary measure, it is useful in the beginning phases of doubles, and to a lesser degree in starting triples. You "salt" to build initial confidence, then reduce the number of dummies used for salting as the dog gains that confidence through success, until they are no longer necessary. Start out salting both areas. As the dog gains confidence, stop salting the diversion bird area, but continue salting the memory bird area until there is no longer any need to do so.

"Rehearsing" is a technique to assist the dog to remember the memory bird. You run him on the memory bird as a single before running the double. After picking this fall up as a single, your dog will more likely remember it as the memory bird of the double. This, too, is a temporary measure which should be discontinued after the dog has shown the ability to remember two falls without it. True, you may use it again when introducing a particularly difficult double, and you will surely use it again in triples. However, it is not a permanent part of your training program, just a temporary crutch for your dog's memory.

"Rerunning" is not temporary like salting and rehearsing. For the rest of your retriever's active life, you should rerun every test he doesn't do perfectly the first time. It is your greatest training tool for marking and memory. That it aids memory is obvious, because the dog surely remembers the falls better the second time. It also develops better marking ability, for the dog gets another look at the falls from the line after he knows exactly where they are.

Rerun every test until the dog does it easily. In simple doubles that normally means just one rerun. Later on, in more complicated work, if the dog is still a bit wobbly the second time, rerun it again—and again, if necessary. If the dog shows signs of tiring before doing sat-isfactory work on a particular test, put him up awhile to rest, then get him out and try it again.

Gradually stretch the distances of the falls to 100 yards or so, always keeping them widespread. Vary the throwing sequence and directions, and vary the length of the falls. Naturally, you should not change anything in one test between runs. That would only confuse your dog. Make your changes between tests.

During this lengthening-out process with widespread doubles, you will probably get a few opportunities to correct your dog for switching (and you should look on them as opportunities, not as problems). In this phase, you are not deliberately tempting him to switch, as you will do later. However, he may take a shot at it occasionally anyhow. Fine, if it doesn't happen too often. Occasional switches are a bonus that give you a head-start on the switch-proofing process. If they happen quite often, you are probably pushing your dog too rapidly.

As soon as he shows competence and confidence on these wide 100-yard doubles, you should set up tests that will strongly tempt him to switch. You have now convinced him that he can handle two falls. Now you must teach him that there is definitely a wrong way to approach doubles, namely by switching.

Shorten up to 30 yards, so you won't have to run so far to cor-rect him. Then, bring the throwers closer together, to where the angle between the falls (birds, not throwers) is about 90 degrees. Then, have both thrown "in" (towards each other). Such throws encourage the switch, because the throwers are not "blocking" the path from one fall to the other. Actually, the throwers never really block that path, but they do constitute some sort of barrier in the dog's mind when they both throw out, for example.

Run this test without salting and without rehearsal. By now a 30-yard double should be easy for your retriever. If he tries to switch, correct him as indicated above, rerun him until he doesn't switch, praise him, and put him up. If he doesn't try to switch, praise him, rerun him, praise him, and put him up. For this latter dog, you should toughen the next test so he is more tempted to switch.

To offer more inducement to the switch, move into heavier

cover, where the dog will have more difficulty finding the birds. He may well search for a while, give up on that bird, and try to switch. Great! Correct him, rerun until he does it right, praise him, and then put him up.

Do not try to make the temptation stronger by moving the falls close together. Ninety degrees is close enough. You want the areas of the two falls to be distinct in the dog's mind. If they are so close together that they overlap, the dog can go from one to the other without understanding what it is he is doing wrong. Incidentally, the "area of the fall" is roughly a circle around the bird with a diameter approximately 20% of the distance from the line to the bird. That is the area in which the dog should normally hunt, and your tests should always be set up so he must go out of the area *significantly* in order to switch.

Intersperse switching tests with confidence builders from now until you have him pretty well switch-proofed. If you can, set up two tests per training session. Make the first a switching test, the second a confidence builder. That way, he will continue to enjoy his work, and won't come to expect to get into trouble every time you take him out. Anytime you must take your retriever through some necessarily negative training, you should see that he gets some positive work along with it, to sweeten him back up. Normally, the positive training should come last, for that is what he will remember next time you load him up for a training session.

The remainder of double marked retrieve training on land consists of introducing all sorts of variations into the tests: cover, terrain, wind, placement and sequence of the falls. You may encounter several predictable problems, so I will tell you now how to deal with each of them.

First, your dog may fail to find one or the other bird. He doesn't switch. He just can't come up with the bird. Naturally, you should let him hunt as long as he does so intently and in the area of the fall. However, when he loses interest and wanders out of the area, signal to the thrower to "help him out." The thrower should do exactly what he did in single marks: Pick up the bird, get the dog's attention ("Hey, Hey, Hey"), and throw the bird straight up in the air so it comes down where it was originally. The thrower should do this until the dog finds the bird. Sometimes he won't see it the first time, or he may forget it again.

Second, your dog may forget the memory bird. When this happens, he may do any of the following things: refuse to leave your side; go a short ways and stop; or return to the diversion bird area. Any of these actions indicates that you have set up a test that is too difficult for him. In other words, this is your problem, so don't punish the dog. Simplify the test.

On the other hand, if you have done all the preliminary work properly, and your dog still has problems, he may have a faulty memory that will never get better. If you suspect this, you would be money (and time) ahead to take your dog to a good pro for an evaluation.

Third, he may break. If you have him on the belt cord (as you should), you can prevent him from succeeding. Just give him a mighty yank, and say NO! HEEL! as you bounce his tush back to the turf. Then, have the throwers pick up the birds and start the test over again. If you have—foolishly—taken your dog off the belt cord too soon and he breaks, you must prevent him from succeeding in making a retrieve somehow. Signal the throwers to pick up the birds, holler NO! HEEL!, chase him down if necessary, but bring him back to the line without a bird. Then, start over—this time with the belt cord on, for crying out loud.

Fourth, the thrower may make a wild pitch. The dummy may scoot along the ground instead of arching nicely against the horizon. It may go straight up and down, landing at the thrower's feet. It may go behind him. Never send your dog after such a dummy in training. Instead, holler "No bird," have the throwers pick up all the dummies, and start over. You set the test up to teach your dog something specific. If the throws are bad, you cannot succeed.

I remember helping a handler with severe tunnel-vision one evening. He couldn't see the falls well enough to call his own no-birds, so I did it for him. The situation was complicated by the fact that his thrower was legally blind. I had to "handle" him verbally to the dummy each time he made a bad throw. If we went to all that trouble to assure the dog good throws, you know it is important.

Fifth, your retriever may develop a "head swinging" problem. He may not watch the memory bird all the way to the ground in his anxiety to see the diversion. This is especially true if the diversion is a shot flier, which excites most retrievers. If he develops a significant head-swinging problem, one that causes him to mismark the memory bird fairly often, a couple of simple things you can do to cure him are:

First, run lots of singles—even set up a double, but run it as two singles. I have never seen a retriever get into a bad head-swinging habit during the time when "rehearsals" of the memory bird were still commonplace in his experience. It is only after doubles are always doubles and triples always triples. He takes a casual look at the memory bird and then turns to concentrate on the diversion. The trouble is, he may not have marked the memory bird well enough to find it. If you set up doubles, but run both birds as singles, he will not be so sure that both birds will be thrown when he sees two throwers. This discourages head-swinging. One important point: If you just run the single, but he swings his head around to the diversion thrower anyhow, don't send him until he pulls back around to the memory bird. You will accomplish nothing by sending him when he is looking the wrong way.

Second, continue to shift your own body between falls and encourage him to follow your lead. Eventually, he will concentrate on one fall until your movement indicates that there will be another. The combination of not always having two birds thrown when there are two throwers in place and using your own body movements as cues will bring head-swinging under control.

Obviously, head-swinging is a field trial and working certificate test problem, not one of the hunting tests, where the throwers are hidden. In the latter, the dog never knows how many falls there will be, so he doesn't swing his head—which indicates the path of correction for field trial and working certificate dogs: Keep them guessing as to how many falls there will be.

WATER

You should delay water doubles until your retriever does quite well in land doubles, for three very solid reasons.

First, water doubles put more stress on the dog's memory than do land doubles. The reason is obvious: Dogs don't swim as fast as they run, so they have to remember both falls longer in the water.

Second, premature water doubles can start a nasty habit of "refusals." Your dog fails to remember the memory bird, so he simply refuses to go when sent.

Even with a large white dummy in open water, he can give you a delayed refusal. Since he can see the memory bird dummy in the water, he may start out towards it. However, after he is swimming, with his eyes low to the surface, he may no longer be able to see the dummy due to wave action or cover between him and the dummy. He may give up, turn around, and come back to you. This can be a nastier type of refusal to deal with than the one in which the dog just sits at heel and refuses to go.

Once your young retriever refuses, you have no good option. If you allow him to get away with it, you give him veto power over your command to retrieve. If you somehow force him into the water, you give him a bad attitude toward water that may color all his future work. It is much better to prevent refusals by delaying water doubles.

Third, you cannot deal effectively with a switch in water. Sure, you can take a shot at diving in, swimming after the errant pup. However, he can out-swim you, so you probably won't catch him. As a matter of fact, you may teach him that he is safe from you in the water, which is something you should keep him from finding out. I have seen more than one retriever high-tail it for water whenever in serious trouble, then swim in circles out of reach of the trainer for a long period of time, simply because the animal knew he was safe there. My golden, Belle, did that to me one time, many years ago.

When should you start water doubles? After your retriever is doing reasonably good work on land doubles in cover, and has been corrected for switching often enough to show that the message is getting through. If, on difficult land doubles, he occasionally starts to switch, then thinks better of it, and returns to the proper area to continue his hunt, he has begun to understand the gospel you have been preaching. He isn't completely switch-proofed yet, but he is definitely beginning to see it your way. He is ready for his initial water doubles.

Start out just as you did on bare ground: widespread (120 degrees); in open water where both dummies are visible; using large white dummies. A barrier would be nice, but you probably won't find one.

You must deal with two conditions here that were not present in your bare ground doubles: drifting dummies, and bank-running.

If the water is choppy, your dummies will drift. This is a problem even on the diversion bird, for the dog swims with his eyes low and cannot see the dummy as he moves towards it. If it drifts, your youngster may fail to find it, even if he goes to the spot where he last saw it. In these initial water doubles, nothing is more counter-productive than "vanishing" dummies.

Running water creates the same problem, so don't start in a river or stream, even if that is where you do all your hunting. Later, after your pup is an accomplished water dog, you can extend his training to running water, and let him become "river-wise." Right now, make everything easy.

If you live in a windy area, as I do, seek out protected coves on big lakes. Sometimes you can find a cove where the water is as smooth as the surface of a chilled martini, even though the main lake a couple of hundred yards away has wildly surging waves.

Another solution, although far less desirable, is tossing the falls on the shore across the water. They do stay put there, and if there is little or no cover on the shore, they remain visible. The dog may lose sight of them as he swims, but at least they won't drift. However, in a strong crosswind, the dog may drift as he goes across the pond. If the falls are short and widespread, this is no problem, but if you lengthen things out too much and bring the falls too close to each other, he could drift into a switch. Bad news. Keep them short and wide.

Even if you manage to stay out of switching trouble, these falls on shore across water are not ideal. They quickly convince the young retriever that all birds fall on land, that water is nothing but an obstacle between him and the bird. That makes him want to run the bank rather than swim. If your dog finds most of his birds actually in the water in his early water tests, he will be more inclined to jump in and stay in rather than look for ways to run the bank.

Later on, you must decide whether you want to completely cure your retriever of any bank-running tendencies. If you decide to do so, you should seek the assistance of a competent pro to guide you through this delicate process (called "water-forcing"). For now, avoid bank-running trouble by setting up tests in which swimming appears to the dog as the only option.

Have every mark thrown so that your retriever can enter the water at pretty close to a right angle to the shore. If, instead, you give him an angled entry, he will tend to drift down the shore rather than get wet. Enough of this nonsense at his young age and he will start looking for a way around the water on every retrieve. Let him "square" into the water until he is handling fairly difficult double marks. Then decide whether to "water-force" with a pro.

Go through all the drills you used in bare ground doubles: different lengths for each fall; different sequences of throws; various throwing directions.

Approach everything gradually, especially length. Many beginners are too impressed with long water retrieves. I have a saying for them: "A short success is better than a long failure."

If, in lengthening things out, you get even a hint of a refusal, shorten up immediately. You don't need refusals now. If you later decide to water-force your dog, the pro will teach you how to deal with them. However, your dog will be older and more experienced then, not a green pup. It is worse than folly to apply water-forcing techniques, which are really strong-arm stuff, to an inexperienced dog that hasn't yet formed his opinion of water work completely.

Use decoys frequently. Granted, putting them out and picking them up is a chore. Nevertheless, your dog should accept them as part of the water working routine, which they are in hunting and all the formal field activities.

On land, you did your bare ground work in parks and on schoolyards, then went out into the country to find cover to work in. In

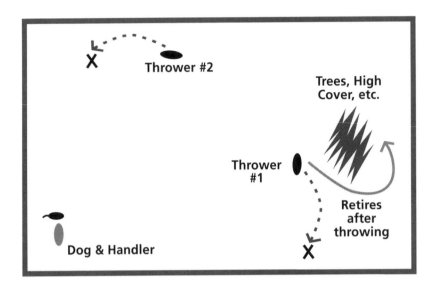

Thrower #2

Trees, High Cover, etc.

Thrower #1

Retires after throwing

Dog & Handler

FIG. 9: Retiring gun test
In a retiring gun test, after the memory bird thrower makes his throw, he "retires," that is, he retreats to a pre-selected location from which he cannot be seen by the dog at the line. This tests the dog's memory because, after retrieving the diversion bird, he cannot use the memory bird thrower to jog his memory about the location of the other fall.

water, the change is more gradual, for you ease from open water into cover in the same training areas, using your own judgment as to when your dog is ready for each step.

As you move into cover, the three techniques mentioned earlier (salting, rehearsing, and rerunning) become important aids. Salting is less useful in water, because it is usually impossible to salt an area large enough to be of much assistance to the dog. However, at times you will have a big patch of cover in the water, where salting may be useful.

Rehearsing does even more for your program in water than on land. Water retrieves test the dog's memory more because of the time it takes to swim to the falls. Continue to rehearse for quite some time. Even after discontinuing it on routine doubles, you should use it when first introducing a new, more difficult test.

Rerunning is your major training tool in water, just as on land.

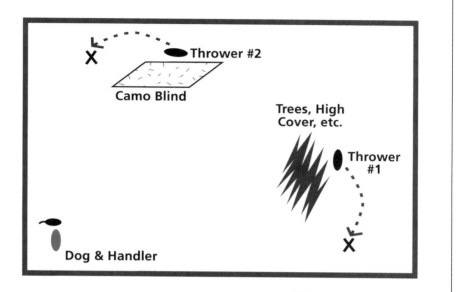

Rerun every test until your dog can handle it easily. Always.

RETIRING GUNS...HIDDEN GUNS

Until now, you have kept your throwers in plain sight. You have brought your dog to the line in a way that has allowed him to locate them easily. The throwers helped him understand the test, and their presence has been a big aid in the development of your dog's memory and marking ability.

However, having throwers in plain sight

FIG. 10: Hidden gun test
In a hidden gun test, the thrower is never visible to the dog at the line. He throws from behind some obstacle, natural or man-made. Here, the memory bird gun is hidden behind some trees or high cover and the diversion bird is hidden behind a camo blind.

to aid in marking and memory is a luxury your dog will not have all his life, whether he becomes a field trial competitor, a hunting test participant, or just a good hunting dog.

If you plan to compete in field trials, you should accustom your dog to "retiring guns." ("Guns" is a synonym for "throwers.") If you plan to participate in hunting tests or just make a hunting dog out of him, you should accustom him to "hidden guns."

"Retiring guns" are frequently used in the advanced stakes of field trials to make the marks more difficult. In a retiring gun double, for example, the memory bird guns remain in plain sight as they shoot and throw, but they hide while the diversion bird is being thrown and shot. When the dog returns to the line with the diversion bird, he no longer has the memory bird guns to mark off of. They are out of sight. Thus, it is a tougher mark.

To train for retiring gun tests, start as soon as your youngster is handling doubles in cover out to 100 yards comfortably, even while you are still switch-proofing him. In fact, the earlier you start, the easier these tests will be later on, for your dog will not form too strong a habit of marking off the guns.

Start retiring the gun on reruns only. Set up a retiring gun test, but first run him on it *without the guns retiring,* more than once if necessary. After he shows you that he can handle that particular test, rerun it a couple of more times *with the guns retiring.* That way, he may be mildly surprised that the guns are gone when he lines up for the memory bird retrieve, but he will not panic. He already knows where the bird is, so the absence of the guns is not a matter of great concern.

If you will do this regularly all through your dog's doubles training—retire the guns on reruns only—by the time you start training for the big stakes, he will be ready to run these tests "cold" (with the guns retiring on the initial run).

The "hidden guns" of hunting tests are totally different. The guns stay out of sight so the dog sees nothing but the birds they throw. Still, you introduce them the same way, on reruns. Start out early in your doubles training using hidden guns *on reruns only,* after your dog can handle the test with the guns in sight. Later, you can sit on a stool and point a shotgun to help your dog see the birds.

HONORING

A retriever "honors" the work of another retriever when he sits quietly while the other dog works. Honoring is required in all age stakes of field trials, in some working certificate tests, and in the advanced tests of hunting tests. Dogs honor on marks rather than blind retrieves because the temptation to break is so much stronger on marks.

In field trials, honoring has become highly ritualized over the years. Your dog works first and then honors the next dog's work. Both the working and the honoring dogs are at the line, each sitting at heel in a designated place, before the birds are thrown. Both must be steady until the judge indicates that the working dog may be sent to retrieve. Once the working dog is well on his way—far enough to have given the honoring dog ample opportunity to demonstrate his steadiness—one of the judges "releases" the honoring dog. The handler heels him back away from the line.

Here's how honoring is supposed to work. Mary Jo Gallagher and her Flat-Coat, Fortune, honor as Marilyn Corbin runs her Golden, Summer. Notice that both handlers are using belt cords. If honoring dog would break, Mary Jo could correct him without out interfering with the working dog.

In hunting tests, honoring has not yet become so ritualized. You may have to honor anywhere, for any length of time, and you may or may not be allowed to stand or sit next to your dog. There may even be several dogs honoring at the same time. The idea, of course, is to simulate actual hunting as closely as possible.

In training you should start honoring as soon as your dog is doing good work on doubles in cover. Run him, rerun him as often

Here Marilyn Corbin and her Golden, Summer, honor as Mary Jo Gallagher works her Flat-Coat, Fortune. Notice that Summer has started to break and that Marilyn is stopping her with the belt cord . . . without making a sound that would disturb the working dog.

as necessary, and then honor with him while the next dog works. Keep him on the belt cord all the time while honoring, even after he is steady enough to be off of it while working.

If you have wisely avoided using the command STAY when your dog is the working dog, you can now use it to great advantage in honoring. Command STAY as soon as you arrive at the honoring position. Eventually, this will tell your dog that he may as well relax, for he isn't going anywhere this time.

The first time your dog honors, he will have no idea what is going on, so he will probably break when the other handler gives the command to retrieve. When he breaks, you have two problems of equal importance: First, you must bring your dog under control and reposition him at your side; second, you must not disturb the working dog with a lot of yelling. Look at it from the working dog's point of view: His handler sends him, and then immediately some guy standing nearby starts yelling at the top of his lungs NO! HEEL! SIT! STAY! GET BACK HERE YOU WORTHLESS SOB! and so on. The working dog will probably return to his handler's side and wonder whether to go the next time he is sent.

If you have the belt cord on your dog—as you certainly should—there is no need to yell. Just jerk him roughly back into the heeling position, and say NO! STAY! *quietly.* That is all there is to it, except that it takes a lot of repetition over a long period of time before your dog will be reliable at honoring, and then fairly frequent brushing up to keep him that way.

When you heel your dog away from the honoring position, always turn towards him as you command HEEL. If you turn away from him, he may take off for one of the marks in a delayed break.

BASIC BLIND RETRIEVE TRAINING— IN PIECES

WHAT IS A BLIND RETRIEVE?

In hunting you will often shoot a bird that your retriever fails to mark. Sometimes he will be retrieving another bird. Sometimes, especially when there are many birds in the air, he will watch the wrong one. Still other times, two or three hunters will knock down several birds simultaneously. If the unseen bird falls right in the decoys, picking it up is simple. However, if it sails some distance away, you need either a boat or a dog that can do blind retrieves to recover it. Personally, I prefer the latter, partially because I am too lazy to row, but mostly because I get a real sense of satisfaction from the teamwork involved in every blind retrieve.

Let me describe what happens on a routine blind retrieve:

You are hunting mallards late in the season on a large impoundment. While your dog is a long way from the blind, chasing down a lively cripple, a fat drake mallard swings by for a cautious look at your blocks. Unconvinced, he angles up and off to your left, so it is now or never. You jump up and shoot three times, slowing him with the first shot and finally killing him with the third. However, by then he is some distance away, and his fall takes him even farther. He finally splashes down stone-dead about 80 yards out in open water and starts drifting slowly away with the wind. By the time your dog returns, the dead mallard is about 110 yards out, still drifting. You heel your dog to the water's edge, face him in the direction of the bird, and tell him that you are about to send him after a bird he didn't see (I use DEAD BIRD for this). He looks intently out on the lake, but cannot see the duck because of the light chop on the surface. When he is lined up in the right direction, you tell him so (I use LINE for this), and then you send him with the command BACK. He jumps in and starts swimming straight towards the bird. However, the duck is drifting, and the dog is drifting. You tried to compensate for this by giving him a slightly false line before you sent him, but there was no way you could be absolutely accurate in this. By the time your retriever is 75 yards out, he is significantly off-line, let's say to the right, so you have to "handle" him (get his attention with the whistle, and then redirect him with an arm signal). You blow a single, sharp blast on the whistle, causing your dog to stop and turn around to look at you. Then, you give him an OVER cast (arm signal) to the left. He turns and swims in that direction. When he is again properly lined up, you stop him and give him a BACK cast (away from you). He turns and swims toward the bird again. Every time he drifts off-line, you repeat this handling process, until he finally finds the bird, which has drifted to about 150 yards out. There he takes it in his mouth and brings it back to you.

You will remember that one bird, and the teamwork retrieving it required, longer than any other bird you shot all day, believe me. You knew where the bird was but couldn't get there, while your dog could get there but didn't know where the bird was. Retrieving that bird took both of you.

The first bird my older son, Bob, ever shot required a blind retrieve. We were hunting doves on a large pond with an island in the middle. For some reason or other, Duffy didn't see Bob's first bird, which fell in the water near the island, about 40 or 50 yards from us. You can imagine the scene. Eleven-year-old Bob was wildly excited about getting his first bird, and anxious to get his hands on it to do all the things an eleven-year-old does with such a trophy—touch it, determine where he hit it, admire it close up, show it off to the other hunters, and so on. If Bob lives forever, he will never shoot another bird as important as that one. We all know how that is.

Well, if Duffy had not been able to do blind retrieves, one of us would have had to swim after that bird. Fortunately, that wasn't necessary. Duffy picked it up in a very routine, almost ho-hum, manner. When I dropped that damp dove in Bob's mitts, I knew that the time I had spent training Duffy to do blinds had just been justified. Ecstatic kid, puffed up dad, and nonchalant retriever.

Duffy once made a convert of a duck hunter who didn't think much of retrievers. You know, one of those "All my ducks fall stone-dead in the decoys, so what do I need a retriever for?" types. He was a damned good shot, and he did kill most of his birds close to his blind, but no one is perfect. One day four of us were hunting together from two adjacent blinds on a big farm pond. We shot several birds from one flock, and while Duffy was picking them up from the decoy area, this anti-retriever guy came to me sheepishly and said, "I scratched down a widgeon that sailed about 180 yards out in the lake. See him out there, belly up?" Standing on a little knoll behind the duckblind, I could make out the white belly of the drake widgeon floating in the choppy water. I lined Duffy up and sent him after it as a blind retrieve. I had to handle him several times because of the wind. The anti-retriever hunter was really impressed—and grateful. He bought a retriever and had it trained professionally before the next season.

As you can see, the blind retrieve is very practical for the average hunter. More than that, it is a lot of fun.

HOW IT ALL STARTED

Dave Elliott was a young professional retriever trainer in Scotland during the 1920s. He competed regularly in British field trials, which were—and are—real hunts in which dogs are judged. No one, not even the judges, knows when a bird will flush or where it will fall when shot. The judges keep several dogs on the line simultaneously. Any judge may ask any handler to retrieve any bird that falls. Since these trials are conducted on well-managed estates with plenty of game, several birds are frequently in the air at the same time. Imagine a line of six or more handlers and dogs walking along, birds flushing everywhere, with shooters killing them regularly. Now, put yourself in the place of one of the handlers when a judge approaches you and tells you to retrieve such and such a bird. Perhaps your dog saw it and perhaps he didn't. Either way, he must retrieve it or be eliminated from further competition.

If your dog fails, the judge immediately asks another handler to have a go at it. If that dog succeeds, his handler is said to have "wiped your eye"—by picking up the bird that you failed to get. "Wiping the eye" of another contestant has always been quite an accomplishment, a significant status symbol. Judges were highly impressed by it, so it was a good way to win field trials.

Naturally, Dave Elliott enjoyed wiping eyes, and hated being the victim himself. However, it was all pretty chancy in those pre-blind retrieve days. Your dog not only had to be a good retriever—marking ability, perseverance, nose, obedience, and so forth—he also had to be fortunate enough to see the fall he would be sent for.

One weekend Dave took a postman's holiday to watch a herding dog trial. He couldn't believe the teamwork exhibited between handler and dog as they moved livestock from huge pastures into small pens. The typical handler stood in one place and directed his dog with whistle and arm signals, thereby helping the dog keep the stock animals in a tight bunch as he moved them towards the pen. Dave was impressed.

On the way home, he wondered if it would be possible to direct a retriever to an unseen fall through similar whistle and arm signals. Without telling anyone what he was doing (in case it didn't work), he started training his retrievers that way. They took to it readily, and before long, young Dave could direct his dogs to falls they hadn't seen—called "unseens" to this day in England and "blind retrieves" or simply "blinds" here—with amazing ease.

After he had sprung this technique on his competition in field trials, he became unbeatable. His dogs picked up all their own birds, by themselves if they saw the falls, or with Dave's help if they didn't. They also picked up the birds other dogs had failed to find with monotonous regularity. Dave wiped a lot of eyes.

The usual responses stirred through the British field trial world. The more reactionary trainers cried "Foul!" while the more progressive imitated Dave's new methods. Eventually, whistle and arm signals were so common at trials that it was not worth entering if your dog would not respond to them. Dave Elliott's discovery was too useful to ignore, so the cries of "Foul!" died away and "handling," as it is called, became part of every retriever's training.

In 1931 Jay Carlisle brought Dave Elliott to this country to manage the famous Wingan kennels. Dave was a major factor in the development of American field trials, so "handling" and "blind retrieves" have been part of them from the first.

Dave Elliott died on November 7, 1985, but he will always be remembered for his monumental contribution to retriever training techniques.

PREREQUISITES

Since blind retrieve training is the most advanced form of retriever training, you shouldn't start it until your dog has advanced into cover in his double marks training. By then, of course, he will have been obedience-trained, force-broken, steadied, and started in switch-proofing. All of these figure in your blind retrieve program, as you will see.

OVERVIEW OF THE TRAINING PROGRAM

You teach blind retrieves in pieces, and then assemble them into a whole. There are only three pieces: lining, stopping, and casting. In lining, you send your retriever on his initial line to the bird. In stopping, you stop him at a distance with a whistle command, so that you can redirect him with an arm or whistle signal. In casting, you redirect your distant dog with arm and/or whistle signals.

The drills by which you teach your retriever to line, stop, and cast bear little resemblance to the end product, the real blind retrieve. A good analogy can be found in football.

At a football team's practice sessions, you seldom see anything that looks much like a football game. Instead, you see calisthenics, wind sprints, running through tires, pushing sleds, hitting blocking and tackling dummies, foot work drills, weight training, and on and on. The uninformed might be tempted to say, "But that's nothing like football! Why don't they scrimmage all the time?" The more knowledgeable understand that football skills and football conditioning are better developed in little pieces and then assembled into a whole. Further, when things break down during a game, the coaches look at the pieces more than they do the whole to find the problem.

You won't hear a coach say to his team: "Well, we lost to old Siwash U. last Saturday because we failed to score from our own twenty yard line the last time we got the ball. Now, men, we are going to drill on scoring 80 yard touchdowns until we get it right!" No, they go back to the pieces instead. The pulling guards work on getting a better angle on the outside linebackers, the quarterback works at smoothing his handoffs, the wide receivers work on more consistent patterns, and so on.

It is no different with blind retrieve training. If you watch a training session, you won't see anything that looks much like those long, impressive blind retrieves you see in field trials, hunting tests, and actual hunting. Instead, you see drills on each of the pieces of blind retrieves. You won't hear an experienced trainer saying, "Well, I blew a trial last weekend because my dog wouldn't do a 200 yard channel blind in a strong cross-wind, so that is what we are going to train on until he gets it down." Nope, they go back to getting all the pieces back in order. Where did the dog break down? How can we fix that piece?

Blind retrieve training, then, begins as a set of drills to teach lining, stopping, and casting separately. In lining drills, called "pattern blinds," the dog is conditioned by rote repetition to leave on command and run or swim in a straight line. Stopping drills are generally worked into basic obedience and then extended through "recreational" hikes with the dog after each training session. Casting drills consist of various "baseball" techniques, so called because the dog sits at the "pitcher's mound" while the handler stands

To set your dog up for a blind retrieve, sit him facing the bird . . . with his head and his spine properly aligned in that direction. Point your toe at the bird so you won't have to glance up to see where it is. Watch your dog's head. When he has the right "picture," confirm it by saying LINE as you put your left hand *beside* (not over) his head. Continue looking at your dog's head until you send him with BACK! Here the author sets his young Golden, Deuce, up properly. *Photo by Theresa Spencer.*

at "home plate" and casts the dog to "first base," "second base," "third base," and calls him in to "pick up a bunt."

HANDLING

Because of the teamwork involved in a blind retrieve, your handling techniques are extremely important.

First, you must tell your dog that you plan to send him after a bird he hasn't seen fall, rather than a mark. I do this by saying DEAD BIRD. Others use "Blind." The exact term matters little, of course, as long as the dog understands it. In hunting he will sometimes see a bird fall dead in the decoys but fail to see the strong cripple that sailed off some distance. You will then want to NO your dog off the mark and send him for the blind first. To do that, you must have a way of communicating to him whether he is to go for the mark or for a blind. Part of the lining pattern training will consist of teaching your dog the meaning of DEAD BIRD.

Second, you must tell your dog when he is lined up properly for the blind. In the lining patterns I explain below, your dog quickly learns to use "pictures" as an aid to running long, straight lines to blinds. When you say DEAD BIRD, he will immediately start searching for the right picture, the right spot to run to, in front of him. Each time he gets the wrong one—and you can tell this easily if you are watching him—you tell him NO. When he gets the right picture, you place your left hand along his head and say LINE to indicate that he now has it. LINE is the normal term used to tell your dog that he is properly lined up, that he has the right picture. Part of the lining pattern training will consist of teaching your dog that LINE means that he now has the right picture, and that NO means he has the wrong picture.

Third, you must tell him when to leave. Personally, I use BACK for this in blind retrieves.

The blind retrieve sequence I recommend, then, is DEAD BIRD...LINE...BACK, each given at the appropriate time relative to the dog's situation. NO is used in place of LINE when the dog has the wrong picture. You normally say DEAD BIRD once. You say NO as often as necessary, whenever the dog shows you he has the

A proper OVER cast. Notice that the thumb is down, which helps keep the arm from flying up too high. Notice also that the author is stepping in the direction of the cast, and that his other arm is tucked in against the body.

wrong picture. You normally say LINE only once, as soon as the dog gets the right picture. Of course, you only say BACK once, immediately after LINE. If you pause too long after LINE, your dog may change pictures, forcing you to start the NO sequence again.

From now on, when I refer to the blind retrieve sequence, I mean: DEAD BIRD...LINE...BACK.

Fourth, you must blow the whistle properly to get your dog to stop, turn, sit, and look at you for arm signals. The dog may be quite some distance away, and the wind may be blowing, so your whistle signal must be very loud. Further, you want an immediate response, so the whistle signal should be short. True, a retriever could be trained to sit when the handler blows his version of "The Old Grey Mare," the Notre Dame Fight Song, or anything else he could make come out of the other end of his whistle. However, to get an immediate response—to get the dog to plant it right there and right

Right: A proper BACK cast. Notice that the arm is straight up, not at shoulder level, not off to the side. Also note that the other arm is tucked in against the body, where it can't accidently send "conflicting messages" to the dog.

Left: A proper COME-IN cast. The author squats a little, toots the COME-IN whistle and moves his arm down a little. The dog will angle slightly in the direction of the arm giving the signal, so use the appropriate arm.

now—the trainer needs a short, easy-to-blow, easy-to-understand whistle command. This stop whistle is the most important whistle command the retriever trainer has, so it should be the simplest. The simplest, of course, is a single, sharp blast—and I mean BLAST, not a sweet warble. Loud, so it will carry a long way.

Fifth, you must give clear, consistent arm signals to your dog at a distance. There are four basic casts: OVER to the left; OVER to the right; straight BACK; and COME-IN. In field trials and hunting tests, experienced handlers give angled BACKs and angled COME-INs that you may eventually want to try. However, in the beginning, stick with the basic four, give them clearly and consistently, and you will be delighted with the results.

You give an OVER by extending the appropriate arm at shoulder level, with the thumb down (to prevent the arm from flying up above shoulder level). Then, walk slowly a few steps in the direction the dog is to go, while pumping your forearm back and forth in that direction. Very clear, easy for the dog to see and understand. As you give the arm signal, you should also command OVER vocally, at least most of the time. However, if you shout it loudly (this is called a "hard" OVER), your dog will go back rather than over. Sometimes this little quirk comes in handy, but more often it is a problem. Form the habit of saying OVER gently (called a "soft" OVER), and your dog will respond better. Later, in delicate situations, where your dog absolutely must not go BACK when you give him an OVER—like when a BACK cast would put him in big trouble—you will give the arm signal with no spoken command. You will find as you go through blind retrieve training that your dog becomes very sensitive to your handling—how loudly you give the commands, how rapidly you move to the side on an OVER, and so on. If you note these things, you can use them to your advantage; if you don't, your dog will give you many unpleasant surprises.

You give the BACK cast by extending either arm straight up so your hand is as high as possible. To ensure that the arm goes straight up and not off to the side, many handlers lock their elbows and swing their arms out in front of them as in a Nazi salute (sorry about that analogy, but it is descriptive) and then on up as high as they can reach.

You must know when to use which arm for the BACK cast. You should always switch arms when a BACK cast follows an OVER—give a right-arm BACK after a left-arm OVER, and vice versa. Your dog will continue the OVER if you give the BACK with the same arm. Also, if there is trouble on one side of the dog, you should give the BACK with the opposite arm. For example, if the dog is sitting on the edge of a hill, and might go down the hill and out of sight if he turns the wrong way, give the BACK with the "uphill" arm.

You give the COME-IN primarily with the whistle, but you should add a little body-English too: crouch a little and extend one arm or the other down.

Sixth, you must make yourself visible to your dog during this training. Field trialers wear white jackets, but that practice has been outlawed in the hunting retriever tests, where handlers must wear dark or camo clothes. Even so, you should wear white while training, especially in the early stages. You can add complications like camo clothes after your dog is fully trained.

EQUIPMENT

You need three traffic cones, the bigger the better. And, please, warm the hearts of the nice folks at your city street department by calling and asking where you can buy them. They are very inexpensive, unless you have to buy hundreds of them, as does your street department to replace the ones that are regularly stolen by otherwise honest citizens for a myriad of recreational purposes.

Your cones will be bright orange, which helps the color-blind canine not a bit. To be visible to your dog, they should be white. You can paint them, but paint doesn't stick too well to slick plastic. It also gets very dirty very quickly. I prefer to have my wife make little white sleeves for my cones. When these get too dirty for good visibility, I toss them in the washing machine. You don't have a wife to make them? Well, although I can't solve all your domestic problems, I can help with this one. Contact the home economics teacher at your local high school. She should know a student who would love to make a few extra bucks stitching up your cone sleeves.

You need some way to mark the location of a blind retrieve so that it is visible to you but not to your dog. Some use little strips of surveyor's tape. I prefer wooden stakes with long nails in one end. I make them myself from 1" to 1.5" dowel. I drill a hole for the nail, pound it in, and then grind the head off so I can stick that end of the nail in the ground. I also drill a hole in the other end, so I can stack these stakes for better visibility in high cover. I make them in various lengths, from about 12" to about 30". You don't have a husband who can make stakes for you? Well, with the disclaimer made above relative to wives, I can help you here too. Contact the shop teacher at your local high school.

These stakes are also useful for marking the line, elevating the cone, and staking out a "baseball" diamond (in casting drills).

Here are two traffic cones and three marker stakes. The left-hand cone has a white cloth sleeve to make it visible to the dog. The right-hand cone is orange, as they come from they factory. It must be painted white or covered with a white sleeve before it is useful for dog training. The marker stakes are orange, which is easy for humans to see but difficult for (color-blind) canines. Each stake has a guttering spike nail in the base so it can be pushed into the ground.

Right: The author prepares to send the Chesapeake, Beaver, in a cone pattern blind on land. Note that the dog is properly lined up, that the author's hand is not blocking the dog's view, and that the author is looking at the dog's head, not the cone.

Left: The author has just sent Beaver to the cone, and the dog is racing there. This drill helps maintain the dog's style and intensity.

LINING
Pictures

You need to understand the concept of "pictures" before you can understand how lining drills work.

On the initial cast in a blind retrieve the dog doesn't—as people thought for many years—"run a line." No, he runs to a pre-selected spot. Think about it: If you were asked to walk 100 steps in a certain direction, you would pick a distant object—tree, building, cliff, etc.—and walk toward it. You could never succeed if you looked at your shoes and tried to walk straight, could you?

A retriever does the same thing, except that he has no idea how far he is being sent. He knows the direction, and after he has run a number of pattern blinds and real blinds, he selects a spot in that direction that his experience tells him should hold the bird. He sits at the line and looks through his "picture album" of past blind retrieves until he finds one that resembles the terrain before him.

The cone pattern blind works in water as well as on land, as the author and Beaver demonstrate here.

If his picture is absolutely accurate, he will run right to the bird, or "line the blind." If it is off a bit, the handler must stop and redirect him. The farther off it is, the more work the handler has to do.

Pattern Blinds

You teach your dog to line by running him on "pattern blinds," which are simulated blind retrieves in which the dog knows where the bird or dummy is, although he has not seen it fall as he would in a marked retrieve. Running pattern blinds conditions the retriever to run long straight lines.

There are several types of pattern blinds. Some of them encourage the dog to use pictures, while one long-popular one does not. Those that do are: cone blinds, floating dummy blinds, sight blinds. The one that doesn't is the mowed path blind.

The *cone blind* surpasses all other pattern blinds not only for introducing the young retriever to lining, but also for rapidly building his picture album in terrain, cover, and wind variations on land and in water. In this technique, you teach your dog that the dummy will always be by the highly visible white traffic cone, that he only need run straight to the cone no matter where it is, and he will find the dummy.

I didn't invent this technique. I learned of it from Margaret Patton of Tishamingo, Oklahoma. She told me that she picked it up from a pro down in Texas, who may have learned it from someone else, and so on. Whoever he was, the inventor of this technique has given us an outstanding pattern blind approach, the best in my experience.

After you have conditioned your dog to run to the cone on DEAD BIRD...LINE...BACK, you can set up a pattern blind anywhere, land or water, and line your dog to it successfully the first time. After he has run it once or twice with the cone in place, you remove the cone and rerun him a couple more times, to condition him to run to a picture without the cone.

The *floating dummy blind,* in which a large white dummy is tossed out in open water before the dog is brought to the line, can only be used in quiet water. However, it does offer great visibility to the dog, and encourages him to work with pictures.

The *sight blind,* in which the handler heels his retriever from the line

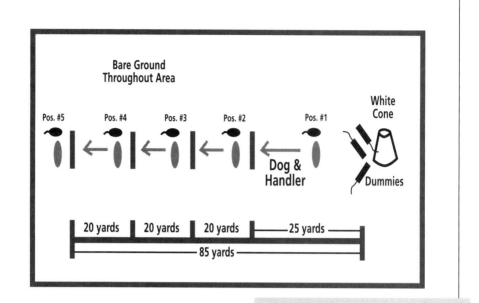

Bare Ground Throughout Area

Pos. #5   Pos. #4   Pos. #3   Pos. #2   Pos. #1   White Cone

Dog & Handler   Dummies

20 yards   20 yards   20 yards   25 yards

85 yards

to the dummy and then back before sending him, encourages pictures. However, it takes too much time, and it cannot be used in water.

The *mowed path blind*, in which the dog is conditioned to run along a path mowed in the cover to the dummy at the end of the path, does not encourage pictures, teaches the dog to run down every cow-trail he encounters, and cannot be used in water. It also limits you to the one area in which you have mowed the path(s) for all your lining drills. Besides, you must spend too much of your training time pushing a lawn mower. Bad technique.

Your Training Program for Lining

You must first let your retriever know that you are introducing him

FIG. 11: Introducing cone pattern blinds

To introduce the cone pattern blind, heel your dog to the cone and toss several dummies near it, saying DEAD BIRD for each. Then heel him back to about 25 yards and sit him facing the cone. Say DEAD BIRD . . . LINE . . . BACK! As he runs to the cone, you should run back another 20 yards or so. When he delivers the dummy, rerun him from there (about 45 yards), and so on out to your maximum distance. After a couple of sessions, he will understand the place of cones in his life, so you will no longer have to heel him to the cone first. Just put the dummies out with the cone, then bring your dog to the line. When he sees the cone, he will know where to go when you send him.

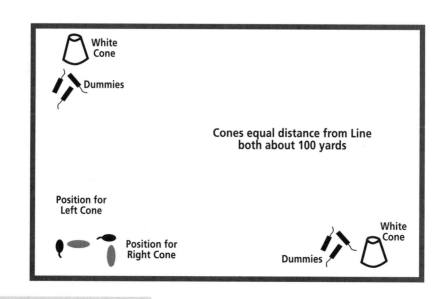

FIG. 12: Initial double cone pattern blinds

Put out two cones with dummies at about 100 yards, with a 90 degree angle between them. NO him off of one cone and line him to the other, and vice versa. This starts the process of teaching him to take the line you give him, even when he knows there are dummies some-where else.

to a new kind of retrieve, one which is not like the marks he has done so far. You must also teach him that the white traffic cone plays a significant role in these new retrieves. Fortunately, you can do both simultaneously.

Not too surprisingly, you start on bare ground. Set your white cone out about 100 yards from your intended starting point, or line. Ideally, the cone should be straight downwind and strongly front-lighted. If both are not possible, favor good lighting over "proper" wind.

Now, grab half a dozen big white dummies and let your dog out of his crate. Heel him from line to the cone and stop. With him sitting at heel, toss a dummy near the cone, saying DEAD BIRD as you do. Toss another dummy near the cone, saying DEAD BIRD. And so on until all six dummies are lying near the cone. Saying DEAD BIRD as you pitch each dummy associates that expression with dummies at the cone. Gradually you will condition him to expect a blind retrieve when he hears DEAD BIRD.

Now, heel your dog back towards the starting point. Stop about 25 yards from the cone, turn to face it, and say DEAD BIRD...LINE...BACK as your dog sits looking at the cone and dummies. Since you are so close and the dummies are so visible, he will run happily to the cone and pick one up.

As he runs to the cone, you should run back another 20 or 25 yards towards the line. That way, when he returns to you with the first dummy, you can send him again from a greater distance, without him noticing the difference. Remember how you lengthened his marks?

Repeat this until you can send him from the line itself, 100 yards from the cone. This may take time. Fine. A short success is better than a long failure. If he is a little wobbly at some length, shorten up immediately. If stretched too rapidly, some dogs, especially the very young and those with an independent streak, may lose their concentration and wander off-line. Don't let that continue. Drill such a dog at a shorter distance for several training sessions. First, drill in the straight line to the cone. Distance can come later.

Don't overwork your dog in any one session. While you stand still at the line, he runs back and forth between you and the cone, up to 200 yards round-trip. If you frequently exhaust him, you may permanently damage his attitude toward blind retrieves. Once he can run straight for the full 100 to 150 yards, give him a drink and a thorough rest after every third retrieve.

After a few sessions, your retriever will recognize the significance of the cone. When he looks for it, and locks in on it, as soon as you get him out of his crate, he understands. Then you no longer need to heel him to and from the cone before you run him.

Change places often. If you can find half a dozen bare ground spots, rotate your training session among them regularly. Also, put the cone in different places and run from different starting points at each location. That will convince the dog that the dummies are always by the white cone, no matter where it is and no matter where he is.

Once your retriever can successfully handle single cone pattern blinds out to 150 yards in several different places, you should teach him that there can be two cones in sight, each with dummies, and that it is YOUR option, not his, which one he is to go to. This teaches him not only to take the line you select, but also what NO means when he has the wrong picture.

Put out two cones with dummies, each 100 yards from the line, with an angle of about 90 degrees between them. The sun should light the two cones equally.

Now, bring your dog to the line and show him both cones. Sit him facing, say, the left one, and say NO softly. Now, reheel him so he faces the right cone. Go through your blind retrieve sequence, sending him on BACK. At that wide angle, he should have no problem going to the cone you selected.

When he returns, sit him facing the same (right) cone. Tell him NO softly. Reheel him to face the left cone. Go through your blind retrieve sequence, sending him on BACK. Again, he should have no problem.

You have started teaching him that even though there are two cones out there, each with dummies, he should go to the one you select. Later, when he gets the wrong picture on a real blind retrieve, you will be able to NO him off of it easily. He may remain convinced that there is a bird where he had it pictured. However, he will understand that you want a different bird, so he will look for a new picture.

Remember to rest him frequently during this two-cone training. Don't get so engrossed in your own success that you forget that your dog is running about 300 yards every time you say BACK.

After several such sessions in different locations, start bringing the cones closer together. 60 degrees. 45 degrees. 30 degrees. No closer than that, please.

What if he veers off and goes to the wrong cone? Handle it like you did a switch in his double marks. Say nothing, but run out and catch him as quickly as you can. If he picks up a dummy, heel him back to the cone from which he got it, take it and drop it by the cone, saying NO rather severely. Punish him according to his temperament right there by the cone. Then, heel him to the cone he should have gone to. Have him pick up a dummy and sit facing the line. Leave him in a SIT-STAY and return to the line. Call him to you, and praise him when he arrives. He must know that you are happy when he brings you a dummy from the right cone, even if you

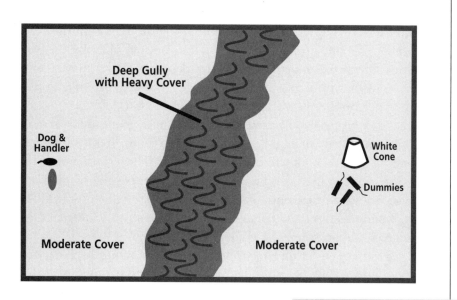

Deep Gully
with Heavy Cover

Dog &
Handler

White
Cone

Dummies

Moderate Cover

Moderate Cover

had to help him. Then, rerun him on the same cone until he gets it right. After that, start rotating him between cones again.

When he can handle two cones at an angle of 30 degrees consistently, start using three cones. Begin with 45 degree angles between adjacent cones. NO him off of two cones and send him to the third. Vary the cones you send him to each time. Then, move them closer together, but not closer than 30 degrees.

While you are teaching your retriever to handle multiple cones, you should also begin accustoming him to the process by which you will later wean him from the

FIG. 13: Cone pattern blind through a hazard
After your dog is comfortable with cone pattern blinds, you can use them to set up pattern blinds in cover with hazards . . . and your dog will do them correctly the first time, every time. This diagram illustrates a cone pattern blind with a deep gully as the hazard, but you can introduce any hazard this way.

cones. Set up a single cone pattern blind with three white dummies and two dark ones. Run him on it twice with the cone in place, and then put him up while you remove the cone, leaving the dummies where they were. In all likelihood, he will have picked up two white dummies, leaving two darks and one white. If not, when you remove the cone, put out new dummies so there are two darks and one white. Now, get your dog out again and rerun him with the cone gone. The one white dummy will be a visual aid, and he will undoubtedly pick it up rather than a dark one. Next, rerun him twice more, with only dark dummies out there. You are encouraging him to use pictures even when the cone is not in sight.

After he can handle these reruns without the cone and also multiple cones, you can mix the two. Set up two cones, 45 degrees apart, and run him on both with the cones in place. Then rerun both without the cones. By this time, he should no longer need white dummies, so use all dark ones. Eventually, you will be doing this drill—rerunning without the cones—with three cones at an angle of 30 degrees. No problem, just gradual conditioning.

Next comes a really major step, and a critical one in giving you the ability to NO him off a picture later on in real blinds. Set up two cones at 45 degrees with dark dummies. Run him on each of them twice. Then, put him up, and *pick up only one of the cones,* leaving the other in place. Now, get him out, and NO him off of the visible cone and send him to the other dummies (without a cone). This could take some time, and some corrections, but it is an important step in training your dog to find a picture along the line you give him.

Repeat this drill every training session. Through it you will gain absolute control over the line your dog takes. You will also, in later real blind retrieves, be able to NO your dog off of any white patch (milk carton, plastic bag, etc.) he may see. You use the white cones first to teach your dog to work with pictures, and then to teach him to allow you to overrule any false picture he may get in a real blind—even if that picture is stimulated by something white.

At this point, you are ready to move into cover on land and to begin water lines at the same time.

In cover you can set up any type pattern blind you want, as long as the cone is visible. Keep them front-lighted or strongly side-lighted. In tall cover, elevate the cones on stakes of appropriate length. Anytime you question the visibility of the cone, squat down and look at it from your dog's point of view.

You should start cone pattern blinds in water quite simply. Here again, a short success is better than a long failure. Since corrections are nearly impossible in water, avoid them. Do your correcting on land.

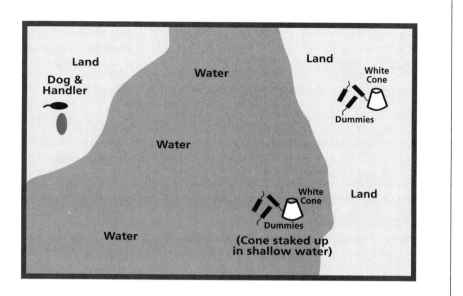

You should place the dummies in the water rather than on the opposite shore, just as you do with your water marks, and

FIG. 14: Cone pattern blinds in water: two set-ups

for the same reason: Dogs that always find the birds on land tend to run the bank. With the cones, you have two ways to keep the dummies in the water. First, you can put the cone on shore with the dummies in the water in front of it. Second, you can stake the cone up out in the water and drop the dummies in front of it. The latter is better, but more difficult and impossible in wind.

Run all your water pattern blinds so there is no real temptation to run the bank. Let your dog "square" into the water, and put the dummies where there are no nearby shores parallel to your dog's path.

Do all the things in water that you did on bare ground: Single, double, and triple cones—but keep the angles at least 45 degrees in water; rerun without the cones; rerun with one of two cones removed; and so forth. Finally, move into cover in water and continue the same basic drills.

You should use a few floating blinds from time to time. They are especially useful in the beginning of these water patterns, and periodically thereafter, to convince your dog that the blind can be a long way from shore. You should do most of your lining work with cones, but an occasional floating blind is beneficial—and easier to set up.

STOPPING

This is really a continuation of the SIT training you have given your young puppy. Even though several chapters have intervened since that initial training, as I stated back then, you should never interrupt that training.

Your pup has learned to sit on either the verbal command SIT or the single whistle blast. That is a good beginning, but you must extend it considerably before you can stop him on the whistle at a distance when he is highballing away from you intent on the spot where he figures the bird is. This extension, again, is pure conditioning, requiring a small amount of work each training session for a long period of time. As a matter of fact, you will never be completely finished until you retire your dog.

Stopping on the whistle is the single most important part of blind retrieve training. If you can't stop your dog, you will not pick up many blinds with him. He can't "line" them all. In fact, even the best lining dogs line very few blinds. Lining and casting are very important, obviously, but stopping is absolutely essential. You can pick up a lot of blinds with a dog that takes sloppy lines and casts if he stops reliably. The reverse is not true.

Fortunately, stopping on the whistle is the easiest part of blind retrieve training, if you are persistent, consistent, and insistent. Let's look at each of these a little more closely.

First, you must be *persistent,* and drill stopping in over a long period of time under every conceivable set of circumstances. You cannot slack off on his training when he does it right once under ideal circumstances. Too many people quit then, figuring that "My dog understands this whistle business now, so let's get on with more challenging stuff." No, dogs never "understand" much of anything in the sense that humans do. They are either adequately conditioned or they are not. If so, they are reliable. If not, they aren't. It's that simple. Conditioning requires frequent repetition over a reasonably long period of time under a wide variety of circumstances. That means that you must persist.

Second, you must be *consistent,* meaning that you must blow the whistle the same way every time. You can't trill the whistle sweetly one time and blast it sharply another and expect your dog to respond properly to both. Nor can you use different types of whistles arbitrarily.

Third, you must be *insistent*. You must punish your dog when he ignores the stop whistle. Every time. You must insist on absolute obedience. If he gets away with not stopping when you are in a good mood and gets clobbered for it when you are not, what is he going to learn? Not much. If you normally overlook two refusals before you go out and correct him, he will learn that the first two toots don't count. Your reaction to refusals must be readily predictable to your dog.

With an attitude that is consistent, persistent, and insistent, you can condition your retriever to sit on the whistle at a distance. Actually, you do most of the training during recreational periods. You should spend time relaxing with your dog, just buddying around, for that keeps the bond between you strong and personal. It takes the edge off when training has gone wrong and there is some hostility between you. Besides, you and your retriever must be buddies if the relationship is to survive. You didn't buy the dog just to pick up birds for you, did you? Naw, you bought him because you like having a dog around twelve months a year.

Go out in the backyard and have a romp with your retriever. Rough-house with him, do whatever both of you enjoy. At some time during this session, when he is highballing the other way, blow the stop whistle. If he skids to a stop and looks at you full of surprise, great! Stand there and praise him lavishly for a few moments, then walk over and pet him before giving him the release command and continuing the play session. On the other hand, if he fails to sit, run him down, drag him back to where he was when you blew the whistle and force him to sit there, blowing the whistle sharply as you do. Then step back to where you were when you first tooted, and praise him—yes, you praise him even though you had to force him to obey. Then, go to him, pet him, and give him the release command.

You can't do this more often than once about every five minutes. If you overdo it, your dog will come to expect it and won't really get into the romping and rough-housing. You want him totally involved in something other than the whistle every time you toot it, just as he will be on a real blind retrieve. If you do overdo it and see that your dog is expecting the whistle, stop blowing it for a few sessions.

Soon he will stop instantly anywhere in the backyard. That doesn't mean he is completely conditioned, but it's a start.

To keep dogs sharp at stopping on the whistle, give them a romp after each training session, and stop them occasionally when they aren't expecting it. Here author stops the Chesapeake, Beaver, and the Golden, Rhett.

Next, extend this to the field by going for a long walk after each training session. While working on bare ground, take a walk around the area with your dog off-lead, if that is safe and legal. If not, put him on a long rope so he can get some distance from you. If you are working in cover, turn him loose for a romp after training. Either way, let him run for several minutes. Then, when he is intent on something else, blow the stop whistle. If he stops, stand there and praise him before releasing him. If he doesn't, correct him. If he is on a long rope, use it to take him to where he should have stopped, roughly force him to sit there, blowing the stop whistle as you do. If he is not on the rope, run him down, drag him back, roughly force him to sit, blowing the whistle as you do. Then, return to where you were when you blew the whistle and praise him. Finally, release him and continue the romp.

Again, you must be careful not to overdo this in any one session. No more than once every five minutes. Surprise makes this training effective. You already know he will sit when he is expecting the whistle.

Repeat this in as many different places as you can, and continue it in all of his training, from single marks to triples and blinds.

If you are training more than one dog, you can work them simultaneously during these recreational romps—after each is reliable on his own. I have frequently taken two, three, or four retrievers for a romp and stopped all of them at the same time, each in a different place in the field, with the whistle. Having canine company tends to distract each dog so that he is less inclined to expect the whistle. It also adds a distraction that tempts each dog to ignore the whistle. However, after one or two corrections, the entire "herd" will stop in synch, every time. Good drill.

That is how you condition your retriever to stop on the whistle. Now, let's look at how you should NOT do it.

Some beginners come up with the bright idea that tooting the stop whistle while their dogs are on the way to or from marked retrieves would be a good stopping drill. On the surface, this may sound good. After all, the dog is surprised because he is distracted by the mark. How better to establish control than when the dog is doing what he was bred to do, retrieve? Besides, there is the productivity angle. Stopping the dog on the way to and from marks is a form of doubling up.

Sounds good, perhaps, but it is a very bad idea. Even if done infrequently, it could slow your dog down on marks. He might start listening for the whistle. Dogs that run very slowly are called "pigs" in retriever circles, and no one wants a pig, so you shouldn't specifically train your dog to be one. Second, your dog will not concentrate on his marks as he should when he knows that the whistle might sound at any time. He cannot develop properly as a marker. Finally, what on earth do you do if he refuses the whistle, especially on the way to a mark? If he gets the bird in his mouth, you can hardly correct him, can you? He would interpret the correction as being for picking up the bird you sent him for, which could start him "blinking," that is, refusing to pick up the bird.

Whistle training can be done so effectively during recreation time that you need not risk making your youngster a blinker and a pig (a "blinking pig?") by tooting the whistle on marks.

Another popular stopping drill gets less attractive to me, at least as an initial training technique, the longer I work with retrievers. That is the practice of working a stopping and casting exercise into your lining drills. To do this, you set up three pattern blinds with angles of about 60 degrees between adjacent pairs. First, you run your dog on each of them until he is comfortable with all three. Next, you send him to the middle pattern blind. When he is about half-way there, you stop him and cast him with a left or right OVER to one of the outside dummies. This is nice, in that it simulates the handling done in a real blind while still doing pattern blind lining drills. It is also productive.

However, it makes the inexperienced dog piggy, especially as he approaches the point where you sometimes stop him. Granted, this can be prevented with most dogs by only stopping them about once in five or six times. However, too many beginning trainers have difficulty restraining themselves this way. They overdo it, even while they believe they are being careful.

It can also start a "popping" problem in a green, unsure dog. A retriever is said to "pop" when he stops and asks for help (arm signals) when the handler has not blown the stop whistle. Every dog will pop occasionally, but with some it becomes a really bad habit. They run a few feet and pop, run a few feet and pop, all the way to the blind. Once started, this habit usually requires the skill of a good pro, or it gets out of hand.

Years ago I started a popping problem with Brandy by doing this very drill too early in his training, and it took the talent of D. L. Walters to bring him out of it. After D. L. cured the popping, I was able to use this drill on Brandy without problem. Still, I could have avoided all the trouble by delaying this drill until he was fully trained. There are better ways to initially condition a dog to stop on the whistle.

This drill—combining lining, stopping, and casting in pattern blinds—is fine for the fully trained dog, the one that has been running real blinds for some time. With such a dog, there is little danger of starting a popping problem or inducing him to run piggy, and it offers a highly productive means of drilling the dog on all three parts of the blind retrieve at once. Since it can be used in water as well as on land, it is an excellent drill for the completely trained retriever, and very productive when you are working several dogs each session. However, it does bad things to the dog that is just learning about lining, stopping, and casting.

Another important part of training a retriever to stop reliably on the whistle comes after he is fully trained and running real blind retrieves. When you get your dog to this point, you will be concentrating on so many other things that you may ease into the habit of accepting a whistle refusal now and then. Wrong, wrong, wrong. Whenever you let your dog successfully slip a whistle, you are training him NOT to sit on the whistle. One refusal today will become two next week, and so on until you join the ranks of the many owners who blow their brains out and then stand there and scratch their heads because their dog just can't be depended upon to sit. "He always used to. Don't know what happened."

Never accept a whistle refusal in training. Never. Hustle out there and make him obey. If you are to do blind retrieves successfully—in field trials, hunting retriever tests, or actual hunting—you absolutely MUST be able to stop him *every time*. The best way to assure yourself that you can is to never let it enter the dog's mind that he can do anything but sit when he hears the stop whistle.

Also, never make your dog regret it when he obeys the stop whistle. For example, don't stop him with the whistle when you want to punish him. If, for example, he switches and you can't catch him, don't stop him with the whistle and then punish him for switching. He will never understand why you are correcting him. He will think it is for the last thing he did, which unfortunately was to obey the whistle. Next time you toot it, he will be inclined to ignore it. Wouldn't you? Instead, run him down, no matter how long it takes.

Occasionally, this training to stop on the whistle comes in handy in a dog's everyday life. Once, many years ago, after a training session, I pulled into my driveway with four goldens (Duffy, Brandy, Mickey, and Pirate) in my little dog trailer behind the car. I let them all out and started toward the backyard, expecting them to follow me as they always did. They didn't, for at that moment a stray cat ran through our yard. All four dogs took off after it. When I saw they were heading for the street, I instinctively blew the stop whistle. Much to my relief (and surprise, I must admit), all four stopped, whirled around, and sat looking at me! The "lead dog" wasn't more than five feet behind the cat when I stopped them, so

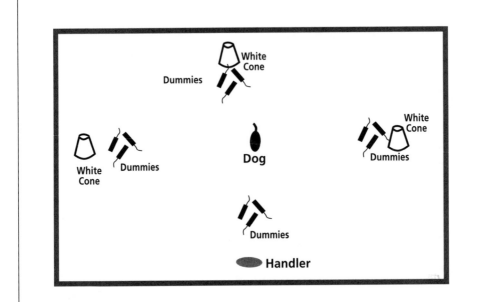

FIG. 15: Basic set-up for cone baseball.

some animal—cat and/or dogs—would have surely been injured had the pursuit continued. If I had ever been tentative in my training on the whistle, at least some of my dogs would have kept on going. I hadn't, and they didn't, and I was kinda proud of all of us as I stood there looking at those four goldens sitting on my lawn facing me. Shocked, a little disbelieving, but proud, too. I walked to the backyard gate, opened it, and—with a nonchalance feigned to impress the neighbors—blew the COME-IN whistle. All four dogs romped merrily past me into the backyard, just as if the cat didn't exist.

CASTING

The Cone "Baseball" Casting Drill

James Lamb Free, in his 1949 classic, "Training Your Retriever," described a very basic "baseball" casting drill. In this technique, you use the positions on an imaginary baseball diamond to teach casting. You place your dog on the pitcher's mound. You stand at home plate. You put dummies at first, second, and third bases. Then, you give your dog arm signals to send him to each of the bases. A left-hand OVER directs him to third base. A right-hand OVER directs him to first base.

A BACK (either hand) sends him to second base. A *come-in* whistle directs him to pick up a bunt between the mound and home plate.

"Cone baseball," which is a combination of Free's basic baseball and the cones used in cone pattern blinds, is excellent for the introduction of the four basic casts. It improves on basic baseball because it offers the visual aid of white cones at each "base."

Your Training Program for Casting

You can do this training in parallel with lining, at least after your retriever understands the significance of the cones.

You should do the initial work on bare ground. Mark out a small baseball diamond with the pitcher's mound only ten yards from the bases. At first, put only one cone out, say, at third base. Now heel your dog to the pitcher's mound and sit him facing home plate. Leaving him in a SIT-STAY, walk over to third base and drop several big white dummies there, making sure your dog sees them. Now, walk to home, turn to face your dog, and give him a left-hand OVER. Having seen the dummies placed there, he should run to third base and pick one up and bring it to you. Repeat this a few times to cement it in. On the reruns, there is no need to walk to third base. He knows where the dummies are. Simply heel your dog to the pitcher's mound, return to home plate, and cast him.

An occasional dog cannot understand that he is to retrieve without first coming to the heel position. Belle was one of these. In her early casting drills, she came to me and then went to the dummy. After several frustrating sessions, I solved the problem by doing these drills on a real baseball field with the backstop between us. I sat her facing the backstop (which was immediately in front of her, blocking her path), and walked around to stand a few feet on the other side, with the cone and dummy at one end of the backstop. She had no way to get to me other than to run around the backstop, which took her to the cone. She caught on fairly quickly. Then, all I had to do was lengthen the distance of the cone from the end of the backstop and the length I stood from the backstop—all the time leaving Belle sitting right next to it, with her nose almost touching the chain link. After many sessions like this, I was able to get her to take casts without the backstop.

Once your dog understands the left-hand OVER, repeat the process with the cone at first base. Then, at second base. Still, keep the casts short, about ten yards, so you can run your dog several times per session without tiring him.

After he has learned to run to the cone no matter which base it occupies, try him with two cones in place, but with dummies at only one of them. That way, if he makes a mistake, he won't find a dummy. Repeat this with the two cones at different bases: first and third, first and second, second and third. When he does this without any mistakes, repeat it with dummies at both cones.

Finally, put cones at all three bases and go through the same drills until he completely understands what is expected of him. Only then, when he can handle both OVERs and BACK (with either arm), should you teach him the COME-IN—which is the easiest cast because the dummy is right in front of the dog in the direction he is facing. After he understands the COME-IN, drill him on all four casts each session, mixing up the sequence so that he never comes to expect any particular cast to follow any other.

Lengthen the casts out fairly rapidly. Twenty-five yards each. Then, 50 yards for the BACK, 35 for the OVERs, and 20 for the COME-IN—and so on until he will do 100 yard BACKs, 75 yard OVERs, and 50 yard COME-INs. That is plenty long enough. Naturally, you can't run him as often on these long casts without rest as you did on the shorter ones.

Change locations every training session. Most city-dwellers have several parks and schoolyards within two or three miles of their houses where this bare ground work can be done, so frequent changes of scenery are no real problem.

Mix up the wind directions, too, so your dog has to go with, into, and across the wind to take your casts. Later on, you will find that it is very difficult to get him to take any cast directly into the wind. He will also drift with a cross-wind. Doing these into- and cross-wind casts with the cones in place as a visual aid encourages him to hold the line of the cast you give him.

After he can handle all four casts at the maximum distances you have selected in several bare ground locations, you should start con-

ditioning him to take your casts without the cones. To do this, you first set the cones up and cast him to each one at least once. Then, put him up for a rest while you pick up the cones, leaving the dummies in place. Initially, use big white dummies because they are so highly visible. Get him back out and rerun him on each cast a couple of times with the cones gone. Since he just finished running each cast with the cones in place, and since the dummies are white, he should have no trouble with this.

> The author gives the Golden, Rhett, a right arm OVER cast in a cone baseball casting drill. The cone marking the dummies for the BACK cast is also visible in this picture. Notice that the author's arm is level to the ground and that he is moving in the direction of the cast. Notice also the enthusiasm of the dog taking the cast.

After he has shown you, during several sessions, that he can handle this drill with big white dummies, start using dark ones. Again, with the build-up you have given him, he should have no problem.

Next try a more demanding drill, still on bare ground. Set up the three cones and run him on each cast at least once. Then, put him up for a rest while you pick up only one cone, leaving the others in place. Now, get him out and cast him only to the dummies without a cone. Do this with each cone position over several training sessions. It will condition him to take your cast, even when there are cones somewhere else and no cone where you are sending him.

I once saw a handler who doesn't train with cones become quite upset at a field trial because there was a white plastic bottle on shore many yards from the location of the bird in the water blind retrieve. He ranted and raved that such a test was unfair because any dog would head straight for that highly visible white plastic bottle. I have also heard another trainer who doesn't use cones claim that using cones will make it difficult to handle a retriever away from any white object that happens to be in the area of a blind retrieve. Wrong, wrong, wrong. If you take the trouble to set up lining and casting drills with cones in places the dog is not to go and no cone where he is to go—as in this casting drill—your dog will be easier to handle away from white objects than will the dog not thusly conditioned. White objects are only a problem to dogs NOT trained with cones.

When your dog is doing both the lining and the casting drills on bare ground very well, move into cover.

Run the same casting drills in cover that you have been running on bare ground. You might start out short, just for a session or two until he becomes accustomed to the new environment, but then you can quickly lengthen him out to your maximum distances. He understands the work already.

In cover, be sure your retriever can see all the cones from his position on the pitcher's mound. If that means that one or more of them must be propped up on stakes, fine. If the lighting isn't right for one cone in a setup you really want to use, simple heel him to that cone and show it to him before you start giving him his casts. This is time-consuming, but you want him to understand exactly where each cone is in all of these cone drills. You are using the picture concept as it applies to casting, so he must know where the cones are to succeed.

Set up your casting drills in every imaginable combination of cover, terrain, and wind conditions. Uphill, downhill, through swampy areas, through trees, with the wind, into the wind, crosswind, through light cover, through heavy cover, through mixed patches of cover, and on and on. You want to condition him to take your cast and run straight through anything he may encounter in field trials, hunting retriever tests, or actual hunting. There is one exception to this: Don't run him through anything that might injure him: cactus patches, barbed wire rolls, broken glass, heavy thorn bushes, and so on. Some may ask what you will do if you run into such circumstances at a trial, test, or in actual hunting. Pro Charlie Morgan gave the definitive answer to that question many years ago: "Even if you are going to have to eat dirt on Sunday, you still shouldn't have to practice it all week, should you?" Actually, with good judges, you should never run into dangerous conditions at any trial or test. If you do, scratch your dog and don't run under those judges again. If you run into such conditions in actual hunting, quite frankly, you have to decide how bad you want that particular bird. Personally, I've never seen a bird I wanted bad enough to risk injuring my dog.

After your dog is handling these cone casting drills in all the cover situations you want to use, including the reruns without the cones and the reruns with only one cone missing, he is ready for water casting. This requires a small pond and a lot of time, but it is worth the effort. Waiting this long to go to water—until your dog is completely reliable on land—has minimized the chances that you will have a problem in water.

The ideal place for water casting is at the tip of a peninsula in the small pond, where the dog has water on three sides. If you can't find such a place, you may have to drill the casts one at a time, starting with the dog sitting on land.

SUMMING UP

After you have done dozens, perhaps hundreds, of lining and casting drills in all the cover, terrain, and wind variations available to you, your retriever should be ready for his first real blind retrieve. I cover that in the next chapter.

However, that doesn't mean he no longer needs lining, stopping, and casting drills. On the contrary, he will need them the rest of his active life. They are not a phase you take him through. They are a way of life for both of you, so don't rush through them the first time, and don't hesitate to return to them whenever he gets a bit sloppy (which he will, believe me).

ADVANCED MARKS AND BLINDS

TRIPLE MARKS
Prerequisites

Many retriever owners stop at double marks, feeling that the time and effort involved in extending their dogs to triples is not justified by the number of occasions on which they put three birds on the ground or water, bang-bang-bang. I shoot a double-barrel, and quite frankly, seldom put down a bird with each barrel. (My two sons, who never remember when I hit a bird and never forget when I miss one, would claim that I seldom put even one down with both barrels followed by a handful of rocks.)

Moreover, some retrievers that do decent work on doubles and blinds just cannot remember that third bird much of the time. Old Duffy was one of them. His major failing as a field trial dog was that I had to handle him to the third bird of too many triples.

However, if you have field trial, hunting test, or working certificate ambitions, you must move on into triples. They are a routine part of every field trial all-age stake, and are even seen occasionally in the derby stake. They are commonly used in the advanced hunting test stakes. Very basic triples are part of some of the working certificate tests.

Besides, the training is challenging. It requires more sophisticated handling techniques than doubles, and greater teamwork between handler and dog.

If you decide to proceed into triples, you should not start until your dog is doing excellent work on difficult doubles on land and in water out to whatever distance you have determined as your maximum—at least 100 yards. By that time, of course, he should be switch-proofed, and he should honor respectably. Although it is not a prerequisite, your retriever has probably had most of his bare ground blind retrieve training, too.

Handling

Once again you should go back to the basic KISS handling system, standing up with your dog sitting at heel. That puts both of you in the best position to learn the intricacies of triple marks.

Later, you can add the gimmicks of hunting tests if you like: sitting on a stool and pointing the gun at each bird; sitting in a blind with your dog outside somewhere; sitting in a boat in open water; in a coffin blind; doing walk-ups with your dog at heel; and so on.

However, don't make the mistake of trying to do all of your training in these exotic positions. Delay all difficult handling until you are putting the final touches on your dog in preparation for those tests, or for some particular hunting condition you know you will face during the season. Initially, train the most effective way: On your hind legs, with your dog's fanny planted next to you.

Your responsibilities as the handler are more complex in triples. Naturally, you still must be sure that your dog locates all three guns before calling for the first throw—and preferably before he reaches the line. You should sit him facing the first memory bird, and shift to face each fall in turn, encouraging your dog with the belt cord to shift with you. In doubles, you shifted once between the two falls. Now you will shift twice, sometimes in the same direction, sometimes once in each direction.

Since there are two memory birds in a triple, and since you should be facing the dog's next retrieve when he returns to you each time, you have to determine in which sequence your dog wants to retrieve the memory-birds before he returns to you with the diversion. This may vary from dog to dog and from test to test. As your dog returns to you with the diversion bird, he will glance, at least once and possibly several times, at the bird he wants next. If you watch him all the way in, you will see this indication of his preference. Then, simply turn to face that bird before he returns to you and you will be properly positioned for his next retrieve.

You will sometimes see a handler, especially in the all-age stakes at field trials, send his dog after the "other" bird second, the one the dog didn't want. That is called "selecting," and it is very useful in the advanced stakes in field trials. However, it has no place in the initial training for triples. Until your dog is competing successfully in at least the qualifying stake, let him determine his own sequence. Don't try to select.

As in doubles, you should only use your left hand when your dog is unsure. If he locks in on each mark, send him with the verbal command only. If he swings his head around uncertainly, place your left hand beside his head, let him lock in, and then send him verbally (without any movement of the left hand). To determine whether he is properly locked in, you must look at him, not at the mark. Sure, you want to see the birds all the way to the ground, but after you have, turn your entire attention to your dog.

One precaution about training for triples after your retriever can do blinds: Resist the temptation to "handle" your dog to marks he has difficulty with. If you make that mistake often, your dog may start popping on marks. If he succeeds in getting assistance this way, his marking will atrophy.

Don't handle on any mark *in training*—ever. You set the test up as a marking test, so insist that your dog complete it that way, even if it takes several reruns before he succeeds.

In field trials and hunting tests you may occasionally have to handle on a mark, just to keep your dog in contention. You are always penalized for it, but usually you are penalized more severely for allowing your dog to roam around outside the area of a fall.

In some working certificate tests, you are not allowed to handle on marks. In others, you may, but you are penalized. Check the rules before running in these tests.

In hunting, you may spook birds by standing outside the blind tooting your whistle and waving your arms, so it is better if your dog picks up his marks on his own. Nevertheless, you sometimes must choose between handling and leaving the bird for the coyotes.

Clearly, then, you can encounter many "real world" situations—whatever your "real world" is: field trials, hunting tests, or actual hunting—in which you should handle on a mark. However, you should not handle on a mark *in training*.

Bare Ground Work

Some trainers have a psychological problem with going back to bare ground for triples after working in cover on doubles for some time. They feel like they are being put back a grade in school or something. I must admit that a lot of dogs have been successfully trained on both doubles and triples without bare ground work. Many pros, who have fantastic spreads for training in cover, do not have ready access to bare ground, so they don't use it. Obviously, their dogs are successful or they would not be able to make a living training retrievers.

However, the average amateur trainer, especially the one with his first retriever, can accomplish more and accomplish it faster if he starts each new phase of his training program on bare ground. That way, the dog learns how to do things right, how to please the boss, with minimal correction. Each phase starts very positive. Corrections, when they become necessary later in cover, will be made against this positive background. The dog will understand what he did wrong, and how to avoid further corrections.

Besides, said average amateur typically has access to more bare ground than cover. There are parks and schoolyards within the city limits everywhere, but finding available cover requires a drive of some distance out into the country, sometimes as much as fifty miles. In the evening after work, you can more easily load up and drive a few blocks to a park than you can head out into the country.

Start out with short, wide triples, using big white dummies on fairly level ground. Twenty-five yards is long enough, and there should be 90 degrees between the adjacent falls. Your dog should be put back on the belt cord, even if he has been off of it for some time on doubles. That third bird may surprise him into breaking initially. Keep him on the belt cord all through the bare ground work, and well into the later training in cover. The best way to cure breaking is to prevent it. The dog that never succeeds in breaking in training—because of the belt cord in all the early stages—will be more reliably steady all his life.

As you progress in these bare ground triples, remember to vary the throwing sequence and the throwing directions regularly. Don't let your dog come to expect the throws in a set sequence every time, and don't let him expect the falls on the same side of the throwers. Mix them up—however, not on the rerun of any one test. Always do reruns with the same throwing sequence and direction as the original test. To do otherwise would be to trick the dog's memory. Make the changes from one test to another, moving to different areas between tests.

Extend your dog's bare ground triples out to about 100 or 120 yards, and mix up the distances regularly: three long marks, two longs and a short, three mediums, and so on. Don't let him come to expect the falls at the maximum distance he can handle every time.

After he can handle all this with big white dummies, introduce dark ones. Continue on bare ground until he can handle any wide triple you can devise with all three dark dummies. Don't try to reduce the angle of the falls to anything less than 60 degrees, even on bare ground.

You will probably get an occasional opportunity to correct for switching. Don't let this surprise you—or upset you—since there is 50% more temptation to switch on triples than on doubles. Make the usual correction, and count yourself lucky for the opportunity.

Wind can be much more significant in triples than in doubles, and if you don't consider it when setting up your tests, you will create all sorts of unintended problems for your dog. As a general principle, set up all your tests with the wind blowing straight from the line to the middle fall. That way it will be quartering away from the two outside falls, and will not carry scent from the wrong bird to the dog as he goes to any of the three. You can also safely use cross-wind tests if you make sure that no deceiving winds are out there to confuse your dog.

Cover and Water

When you move into cover for triples, you do the same things you did for doubles. Shorten up substantially; widen out to 90 degrees again; stay in light cover at first. Lengthen, and add other complications (cover, wind, terrain) gradually, only as your dog shows he can handle them. Use the three techniques—salting, rehearsing, and rerunning—much as you did in doubles. Salting should be limited to the two memory bird areas. Rehearsing in triples normally means running the two memory birds as a double before running the triple. Of course, rerunning is the most significant, and the only permanent one of these three techniques. Use it on every test.

Keep these triples well within your dog's capabilities at all times, extending slowly. Progress through success is not only more enjoyable for both of you than the greatly overvalued "trial and error," but it is also faster in the long run.

Vary everything from test to test: length and sequence of the falls, throwing directions, terrain, cover conditions, wind direction, angles between the falls (although you shouldn't go less than 45 or more than 90 degrees until your dog is quite well trained, and until you are sure you know what you are doing and why).

Have your dog honor frequently. Keep him on the belt cord until you are sure of him, even if he has been off of it for doubles, since triples offer so much more temptation to break.

Introduce retiring guns and hidden guns the same way you did for doubles—on reruns only.

As in doubles, water work in triples should lag behind land work for several reasons. First, water triples put more stress on your dog's memory. Second, you should keep all water work as positive as possible. Third, you can't really prevent or correct switches in water. Even the dog that seems completely switch-proofed on doubles will occasionally have a relapse when there are three birds out there to choose from.

After you have moved into cover, and after your dog has demonstrated that he understands that he is not to switch on land triples, you may safely start water triples. The process is the same as it is for land triples: Short, wide open water triples on quiet water with big white dummies at first; then, extend the length and complexity, first with white, then with dark dummies, until your dog can handle angles down to 60 degrees and falls out to about 100 yards in open water; then shorten up and introduce cover, one mark at a time (one memory bird in cover, the other two falls in open water, then two and one, finally three in cover).

Whenever possible, keep all marks in the water rather than on shore across water—for the same reasons you did this in doubles training. This is sometimes difficult, especially when you are using cover. If you find cover in water a long ways from shore, use it if you have some way of getting your throwers out there. Either a small boat or one of the "belly boats" used by fishermen is ideal. Setting up tests and changing throwers takes more time, but the results usually justify the effort.

Set up your tests with little or no temptation to run the bank. Your dog should be able to enter the water at nearly a 90-degree angle on every mark, and there should not be any inviting shores too close to his paths to and from the falls.

Set up triples in which there is a mixture of falls (two on land and one in water). You could start out with a normal land double followed by a short open water third diversion. Later, you could put one memory bird on land, the other in the water, with the diversion on land. Eventually, you should work up to two memory birds in the water with the diversion on land, which can be a tough test.

REAL BLIND RETRIEVES
Prerequisites
There are two types of blind retrieves: "cold" and "mixed." A cold blind is one in which one or more blinds are run by themselves. A mixed blind is one in which one or more blinds are run in combination with one or more marked retrieves. A "cold water blind" is a water blind retrieve without any marks. The word "cold" doesn't refer to the water temperature.

The blinds in mixed tests are more difficult than would be the same blinds if run cold. The marks offer "suction" to the dog, in that after retrieving the marks, he will be tempted to return to the area

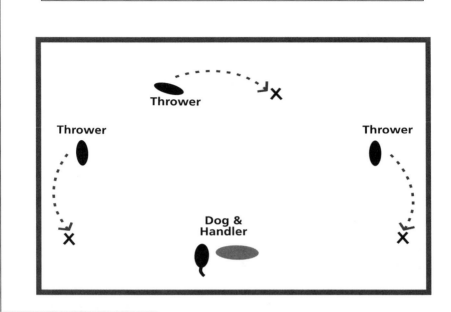

FIG. 16: Widespread triple mark

This is a basic, widespread triple mark. There are six possible throwing sequences: lmr (left-middle-right), lrm, mlr ,mrl, rlm,

of one of the marks when sent after a blind. When a dog does this, he is said to "suck" back to the marks. Because mixed blinds are more difficult, you should delay introducing them until your retriever is well advanced in his cold blind training. First, teach single cold blinds, then multiple cold blinds, and finally mixed blinds.

Blind retrieve training is pure conditioning, and that means lots of rote repetition on the same basic exercises. The initial exercises, of course, are the lining, stopping and casting drills covered in Chapter Seven. You must repeat them and repeat them and repeat them—in many places, under many different conditions—until your dog is fully conditioned. Not only that, but to prevent him from becoming piggy on his blinds, you should under-work him in each session. Thus, the conditioning process takes time.

That frustrates many beginners, understandably. They want their dogs to do those fantastic blind retrieves they see other (fully trained) retrievers do at trials, tests, and in training sessions. Being a little frustrated at what seems like slow progress is understandable, but jumping ahead and starting real blinds too soon is not. Besides, that usually takes longer overall than waiting until the dog is ready.

Reflect on the following fact anytime you are tempted to rush into real blinds: You will never be finished with those lining, stopping, and casting drills; they will be part of the dog's training regimen for the rest of his active life. Every well trained retriever, even Field Champions and National Field Champions, run pattern blinds, stopping and casting drills every week. Again, it's like a football team. The players don't stop doing cals, pushing sleds, hitting dummies, running wind sprints, and so forth, after the first game of the season is behind them, do they? Of course not. They do these things every week during the season—much more than they scrimmage, as a matter of fact.

Years ago a friend of mine asked if I would work her dog for two weeks while she and her husband went on vacation. Some trials were coming up so she didn't want her dog to sit idly in its run for those two weeks. I agreed to because I was familiar with the animal. Even so, it took the dog some time to adjust to me, so I couldn't do anything too fancy with him. I decided to give him nothing but simple marks and the basic lining, stopping, and casting drills. That is all I did with him for two weeks. When his owner returned, she was amazed at how well he did on real blinds—much better, she said, than he had done for many weeks. She asked what I had done, and didn't really believe me when I told her. She just knew that I had worked some secret magic on her dog, and that I was being coy.

Don't think that once your retriever successfully runs a real blind—or 1000 real blinds—you can dispense with the lining, stopping, and casting drills. The only difference then is that you train him on real blinds, too, even though most of your work is still with the cones. Football teams do scrimmage sometimes, and you will train on real blinds—in about the same proportion.

When do you attempt that first real blind? When you are sure your dog is ready for it, not before. When you have drilled him on the cones under all conditions you can think of—many times each. When you are absolutely sure that when you say DEAD BIRD...LINE...BACK, he will leave and run in a straight line simply because he has done it so often that the thought of NOT doing it just won't enter his head. When he will stop on the whistle under any circumstances. When he will take your casts by rote without even thinking about what he is doing.

Transitional Drills

You should use two transitional drills, one for land and one for water, to ease your retriever into real blinds.

The Dummy-String Blind assures your dog success on his early land blinds. In light cover, string out a couple dozen dummies in a 20 yard straight line. I prefer to mark each end of the string with an orange stake, so I know where it is from a distance.

Starting no more than 20 yards from the string, and facing perpendicular to it, you run your retriever on his first real blind. If he runs 20 yards (which he should by now), he will find a dummy on his initial line. As he goes, you run back several yards and rerun him from the greater distance, and so on out to about 100 yards.

The Thrown Blind is the transitional drill for water. In it, you hide an assistant somewhere near where the blind is to be. After you send your dog—with no dummy in place—you signal to your assistant and he throws a dummy so that it lands where the blind should be. That way, your dog leaves and goes whatever distance you feel he can handle on his own. When he starts to waiver, you have the dummy thrown so he can see it in the air in front of him, which encourages him to keep going.

Although excellent for water, the drill is not satisfactory for land. In water, the dummy remains visible after it is thrown. On land, it may be hidden by cover or terrain, making your dog hunt for it like a mark. If he forms the habit of hunting on blinds, he will be very difficult to handle.

Your Training Program for Cold Blinds

This is about the only training for which you don't return to bare ground. You can't, because the dog might see the dummies from the line.

Start land blinds first, using the dummy-string technique in light cover. Start out at about 20 yards and extend to about 100 or so in

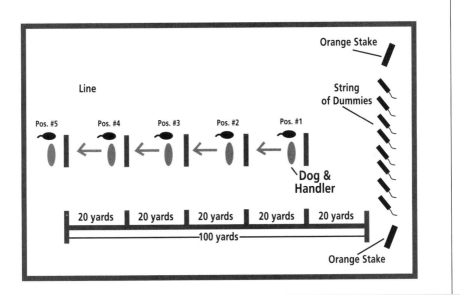

the first session, which shouldn't take more than five or six retrieves. In your next session, go to a new location and set up the string of dummies. This time start at about 40 yards and lengthen out to about 150 yards. Each session you should go to a new location and start from farther back. When you can start at 100 yards, you should make your string of dummies longer, perhaps 35 or 40 yards, to make sure your dog doesn't miss it altogether if he gets a little off-line. It is more important for him to run 100 yards and find a dummy than it is for him to run a precise line at this point in his training. You are trying to convince him that if he runs far enough, he can find a dummy. Once he really believes that, you can work on straighter lines.

In all your dummy-string drills, you do not want to have to handle him (stop him and cast him). Therefore, you should make

FIG. 17: Dummy string blind
This illustrates the dummy-string transititional drill for land blinds. In light cover, lay out a dense string of dummies between two orange marker stakes. The orange stakes tell you where the string is but don't help your color-blind dog. Heel your dog to a position about 20 yards from the middle of the string and send him with your normal blind retrieve sequence. As he goes, you should run back another 20 yards or so. When he delivers to you, rerun him from there (about 40 yards), and so on out to your maximum distance.

these tests as simple as possible—straight downwind, light cover, perhaps a little downhill—to encourage him to run long and straight. If he fails on the first attempt at some distance or other, you have pushed him too fast. Shorten up, so you can avoid a hassle during this transition period, when your main goal is to build his self-confidence.

You can start thrown blinds in water as soon as he can do a 100-yard dummy-string blind on land. Have the dummy thrown in open water, never in cover, where your dog would have to hunt for it.

Keep your assistant completely hidden from your dog's view through this training. If the dog sees the thrower at any time—from the line, on the way out, when the dummy is thrown, or when the dog returns—he will associate him with the thrower in marked retrieves. That will complicate your training program when you get to mixed blinds and marks. I failed to take that precaution with Duffy, and he developed a serious suction problem in mixed retrieves. He wanted to return to the marks when I tried to send him for the blind.

Initially, signal for the throw right after you send your dog. On the rerun, wait until he gets to the water's edge. On the next rerun wait until after he swims a short distance. And so on until he will swim all the way before it is necessary to call for the throw. Of course, rest him whenever he needs it. He swims a long ways out and back every time you send him.

In your second session, don't call for the throw the first time until your dog is at the water's edge. In your third session, wait until after he swims a short distance, and so on. This will build his confidence that the dummy will always fly eventually if he just swims far enough.

After that, change locations often for these thrown water blinds, and delay signaling for each throw as long as your dog is swimming purposefully in the right direction.

When he will run 100 yard dummy-string blinds on land, and is well started in his water thrown blinds, he is ready for more advanced work on land.

Next, run him on a real blind with all the dummies in one place rather than strung out. Since you may have to handle him, mark the dummies' location with something you can see that your dog can't (orange stake or piece of surveyor's tape). Make it a very easy blind, no more than 75 yards long, straight downwind, in light cover, perhaps even downhill a little.

Even with all those simplifying features, he may not hold his original line well enough to find the dummies without help. Great. That's just what you want, so you can handle him.

No matter how poor his initial line is, let him run for at least 50 or 60 yards before stopping him with the whistle. In training, you shouldn't interfere with a dog on a blind right after he leaves your side, lest he think he erred in leaving, which could cause him to refuse next time.

After you stop him, make sure he locates you before you give him a cast. When you have his attention, give him the appropriate cast—typically an OVER one way or the other—*exactly as you have been giving it in casting drills.* Don't let your own excitement affect your movements or rhythm.

If he takes your cast, great. If he fails to take it, stop him again, let him sit and look at you a few seconds to clear his head of extraneous ideas, then give him the cast again, very clearly. He will surely take it if you have done the basics thoroughly enough in the casting drills. When he gets back to the correct line, stop him again and give him a BACK cast (with the arm opposite that with which you gave him the OVER).

On a simple blind like this, you should be able to put your dog on the dummies with a couple or three handles. When he brings you the dummy, praise him like no other dog had ever done anything so wonderful in the history of the world.

Then, rerun him two or three times. You always rerun blinds, just as you always rerun marks—but for different reasons. In marks, you are trying to sharpen his marking. In blinds, you are encouraging pictures. After he has run the blind and knows where it is, he sits at the line again and formulates a picture of it. Lining the blind on the rerun reinforces the picture. Reruns build pictures, just like pattern blinds do.

The rest is obvious: Continue running real land blinds that are well within your dog's capabilities, toughening them up only as he

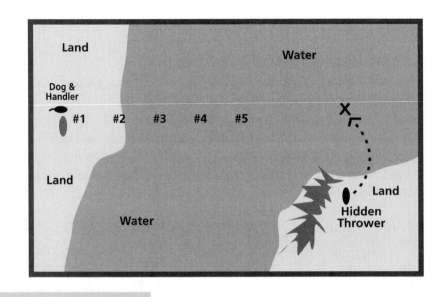

FIG. 18: Thrown blind (for water only)
This diagram illustrates the thrown-blind transitional drill for water. Your well-hidden thrower should throw only when you signal him. Initially, say DEAD BIRD . . . LINE . . . BACK! and signal immediately for a throw. Your dog will jump in, swim out, and get the dummy. Next time delay signaling for the throw until your dog reaches position #2 at the edge of the water. Then delay until he has swum a short distance, to position #3. And so on.

shows he can handle more advanced work. Continue with the thrown blinds in water until you are sure—judging from his land work—that he will respond to handling in water well enough to risk a real blind there.

The extension into multiple cold blinds, in which you plant two or more blinds in different locations and handle your dog to each in turn, is obvious. Start short and wide, NO the dog off the first one before sending him for the second, and correct him like in switching if he returns to the wrong area. Multiple cold blinds constitute an intermediate step between single cold blinds and mixed blinds.

Of course, you should continue the normal lining, stopping, and casting drills. In each training session, run him on a real blind first, with appropriate reruns. Then, go to another area and give him a new cone pattern blind, preferably multi-spoked, first with cones and then without them. This will give him more pictures for his "album." Rest him, and then run him on a cone baseball drill. If you don't have time for both lining and casting, alternate the two in your sessions. After each session, go for a walk and stop him once about every five minutes.

Problems in Cold Blinds

There are three major problems you can encounter as you run your dog on real blind retrieves: poor initial line, refusing, and popping.

Poor Initial Line (PIL): At some time or another in a real blind, your dog is going to think he has a better idea than you have. You will sit him facing the blind and try to get him to line up on it, but he will look some other way. When this happens, reheel him facing the direction he is interested in and say NO, just as you have been doing when selecting one cone from the several you put out in the lining drills. He should understand that this means you are vetoing his idea. Then, reheel him to face the blind again and try to line him up on it. If he still looks the wrong way, put your hand down just as if he were looking in the right direction and send him. He will go the wrong way, of course, and you should let him go that way for at least 50 or 60 yards. Then, get out there and correct him firmly and bring him back to the line and start over.

As I have mentioned before, dogs are very place-conscious when it comes to punishment. Your dog will not want to return to where you just corrected him, so when you rerun him he will be more inclined to listen to your NO and then take the line you give him. First, sit him facing where you just clobbered him and say NO firmly but quietly. Then, reheel him and sit him facing the blind and go through your blind retrieve sequence. He will probably take your line this time. In fact, he may even over-correct and take a line too far on the other side of the line you gave him. If he does this, let him run 60 yards and handle him to the blind. He was trying to obey. In fact, he was trying too hard.

Gradually, your dog will come to understand that his NO training extends to pictures he gets on real blinds as well as to the ones you gave him with the cones.

How far off-line is too far off?

Initially, err on the side of leniency, lest by correcting him too often you cause him to refuse to leave your side on BACK. For quite a while, ignore a line error of up to 30 degrees. Getting him to run long and straight, and building his confidence are your first concerns. Later, you can tighten up your requirements as to the precise direction he takes. You do this by running him on multi-spoked cone patterns with angles between adjacent legs that approximate the degree of accuracy you are striving for. NO him off one leg and send him down the other, just as you have been doing with the larger angles so far. Only after your dog has had plenty of work on these cone pattern blinds can you correct him for being off-line by the same angle in real blinds.

How severely should you punish him for PIL?

That, of course, depends on your dog's temperament. As in switch-proofing on marks, his innate place-consciousness relative to punishment gives you a built-in gauge. If, on the rerun, your dog takes the same bad line, you have not been heavy-handed enough. On the other hand, if he refuses to leave your side on the rerun, you have been substantially too rough with him. If he takes a line which is quite bad on the other side of the line you are giving him, you have laid-to somewhat more than he can handle. Obviously, if he takes approximately the right line on the rerun, you have done it about right.

This place-consciousness has significant implications for you in determining how far off-line is too far. You should always correct him about 50 or 60 yards from the starting point, so the spot at that distance on his wrong line must be far enough from the true line so the dog can understand the difference. If you feel that he will avoid the true line on the rerun because he was corrected too close to it, you either have to accept his line, lighten up on the correction, or let him run farther out before you correct him.

Refusal, here, means your dog remains at your side when you command BACK. There are other forms of refusals—whistle refusals and cast refusals, for example—but here we are speaking of refusing to leave when sent on a blind retrieve.

You should determine why he refused before trying to correct the problem. If you have rushed him into real blinds, he may be so uncertain of what you expect that he freezes at your side. Or, if you have punished him too severely for PIL, he may have decided it is safer by your side.

If you have rushed him too much, the solution is obvious: Back off awhile, and do the basics more thoroughly.

If you have over-corrected him, the solution is also obvious: Go back a few spaces, start again, and when he makes a mistake, go a little easier on him.

If you are convinced that neither of the above causes is responsible for your dog's refusals—or if the habit has become so ingrained that he doesn't respond to the above approaches—HIE THEE TO THY PRO with all possible alacrity. You need the kind of individual direction that only a pro can give you, and the longer you wait the more difficult your dog's problem will be to cure.

Popping is stopping and looking for directions before you blow the whistle. The dog that does this is uncertain, and has probably been handled too much too soon, again indicating that real blinds were started before the basics were drilled in well enough.

Every dog will pop occasionally, but if yours is doing it frequently, you have a problem worth worrying about. Popping can become a nasty habit in which the dog won't go more than a few yards on his own without stopping and asking for help. However, it doesn't start out that severe. The trainer has to really work at it to make it that much of a problem.

When your dog pops occasionally, ignore him. Wait him out. Look the other way. Do anything except give him the arm signal he wants. If he is tough enough, you might even run towards him as if you are going to punish him. The important thing is to avoid giving him that arm signal.

Run him on a lot of cone pattern blinds to build up his confidence. The cones encourage him to use pictures, and a picture encourages him to run to a certain spot on a blind, rather than ask for help. Thus, pictures, and the cone pattern blinds that encourage them, are preventatives and cures for minor popping.

What if that doesn't solve the problem? Well, popping has ruined

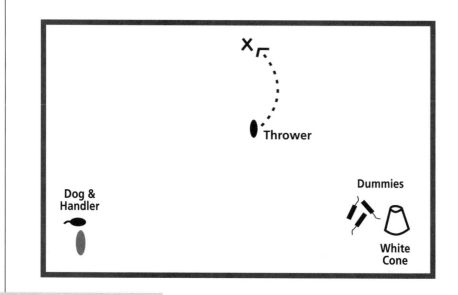

Dog &
Handler

Thrower

Dummies

White
Cone

FIG. 19: Single mark and single blind retrieve
To start your dog out on mixed tests, run your dog on a 100-yard bare-ground pattern blind with the cone in place. Next, set up a single mark off to one side, at an angle of 45 to 60 degrees. Run him on the mark, then NO him off the thrower and run the same blind.

a lot of good dogs, so you should not waste much time on it. If your dog doesn't come around quickly, get him to a pro—pronto.

MIXED MARKS AND BLINDS
Prerequisites

While you are working your dog on cold blinds, you should also do the preliminary conditioning for mixed marks and blinds. Do this in conjunction with your regular cone pattern blinds.

Set up a 100-yard pattern blind and run him with the cones in place once or twice. Then, set up a simple 50 yard single mark at a 45 to 60 degree angle away from the line to your cone blind. Run him on the mark. When he returns, sit him facing the mark and tell him NO—this is very important—and then reheel him and sit him facing one of the cones. Go through your blind retrieve sequence and send him for the blind. Since he has already run it, and since the cone is still there, he should have no difficulty with it.

Now, put your dog up for another rest, while you go out and pick up the cone. Naturally, you leave the dummies in place. Get your dog out again and rerun the entire test, mark first and then the pattern blind. Again, since he has run the test at least twice, he should have no trouble with it.

When he can handle it, add a second mark, then a third mark, then a second blind. Take your time and let your dog succeed as much as possible.

However, at some point in this training, your dog will suck back to the mark. The correction should be similar to that for switching, for the mistake is similar to switching. When your dog sucks back to the mark, let him go all the way to the area of the mark and correct him right there. Since he has already retrieved the bird, he cannot suck back successfully. Go out there, run him down and bring him back to the area and correct him appropriately. Then, take him back to the starting point and run him on the blind again. After he runs it successfully twice, rerun the entire test, mark and blind.

As in the correction for switching, your dog's reaction on the rerun will tell you whether you are correcting properly.

After you have run him on mixed tests incorporating every cone pattern blind you normally use—often enough and in enough places to prove that he understands that suction is a no-no—use the transitional techniques (string of dummies, and thrown blinds) to introduce real mixed blinds. After he has shown he can handle these, go ahead and start real mixed blinds—just as you did real cold blinds.

BEYOND TRIPLES AND REAL BLINDS
Water-Forcing

So far, you have avoided "the occasion of sin" relative to bank-running, lest in correcting your pooch for "cheating" (as many call it) you start a nasty habit of refusals, in which he stays at your side after you send him to retrieve. However, to advance beyond where you have brought your dog now, you must convince him that he should take straight lines to every mark, to every blind, even if he sees a more enticing path.

You could stop here and have an outstanding working retriever.

However, he won't do well in field trials or the more advanced stakes of hunting tests. The judges set up tests to tempt the dog to run the bank, and mark him down if he does. Even in ordinary hunting, your retriever will fail to find some birds if he runs the bank, especially if obstacles and the terrain lead him into a no-man's land completely away from the water.

It's your decision, and now is the time to make it. You can leave him as he is or you can water-force him. If you decide to do the latter, enlist the assistance of a good pro. Either let him do it or let him guide you through it.

Water-forcing is not a quick-fix process. It is an integrated training procedure requiring some form of heavy artillery, like the electronic collar. Done properly, such artillery doesn't damage the dog's spirit (or his body). However, done carelessly, it can ruin the dog. With the training he now has, your retriever may be worth several thousand dollars. Don't squeeze nickels on his water-forcing. Find a pro you trust, and pay the man.

Talk to several pros before you decide. Then, if you decide to do it, don't stop half-way. A half-water-forced retriever is worse than one that runs the bank with abandon.

Quadruple Marks

If you plan to run field trials, you will have to train your dog to do quads before entering him in his first amateur or open stake. Eventually, they will extend things to quints—many serious trainers are already throwing the fifth bird in training.

If you decide to go on to quads, the procedure is similar to that for extending from singles to doubles and doubles to triples. Bare ground, big white dummies, and so forth. However, quads are significantly more difficult than triples. Think of the increased number of throwing directions and sequences.

Selecting

Now that your retriever handles triples well, you should start selecting with him sometimes. By that I mean, you should send him for the birds in a sequence different from that which he would choose.

Like so many other things, start selecting on reruns only. That way, he knows where all the birds are, so will be less apt to fail, less apt to switch. When you feel he is ready for selecting on the original run, shorten up and simplify the marks. Even after he understands selection well, don't do it too often on the initial run in training, just enough to keep him sharp.

ADVANCED HANDLING
Marked Retrieves

In field trials, hunting tests, and working certificate tests, you have two major decisions to make about how to handle any given multiple marked retrieve: Whether to select, and whether to handle on a mark.

You should make your decision on selection based on your assessment of how your dog can best pick up all the marks without having to be handled. If you feel he can do that most easily by retrieving the falls in the sequence he prefers, let him do it that way. If you feel that selecting will increase his chances of picking up all the meat without handling, you should select. For example, if the two memory birds are "snug" (close together) and the diversion is off some distance to one side, you should probably select the middle bird first. That way, he only faces a widespread double after he delivers the first bird. If he were to retrieve the diversion first, he would face a tight double, on which he might well require handling. Another example: If one of the two memory birds is significantly more difficult than the other, you might choose to select it (the tougher one) after your dog picks up the diversion.

In actual hunting, you may select or not select according to your assessment of the best way to fill the freezer. For example, if one bird is a strong cripple, you should select it first regardless of the order in which it was shot.

All of this assumes that you have selected in training long enough to be comfortable with the probable results. If not, take your chances with his natural sequence.

Your second decision, whether to handle, is more complicated.

Contrary to the opinions of many whistle-happy novices, handling on a mark is not a meritorious thing. It means that your dog has failed to mark and remember the bird. Thus, you should not handle unless you have no other choice.

In training, don't handle, period. If your dog can't find the bird, have the thrower help him out. Don't risk starting a popping problem.

In hunting, allow him plenty of time to find it on his own, lest you damage his initiative and start a popping problem. However, as soon as he convinces you that he has lost his mark, toot your whistle and handle him quickly to the bird, so you can get back to hunting.

In field trials and hunting tests, as soon as your dog has shown the judges that he has lost his mark, handle him. Highly respected judge Darrell Kincaid had a saying for handlers who refuse to toot the whistle under such circumstances. "You are allowed two mistakes, and you've just had both of them. First, your dog showed me he can't mark. Second, you showed me that he won't handle either." With that he tore your sheet out of his notebook, r-r-r-rip.

In working certificate tests, you may not be able to handle on a mark. It may be against the rules. However, if it is allowed, handle when the dog is clearly lost.

A dog has lost his mark when he spends a significant amount of time outside the area of the fall. How large is that area? It varies with the length of the fall, the sequential number of the fall, the cover and terrain and wind conditions—and the eyes of the beholder. Again, the following is a good rule-of-thumb definition: The area of the fall is a circle around the bird with a diameter roughly 20% of the distance from the line to the fall.

Once you start handling on a mark, continue handling until your dog picks up the bird. Don't let him resume hunting on his own. Whistle and cast him to the bird as quickly and directly as you can.

Blind Retrieves

To succeed in field trials and hunting tests, you must understand the "fairway" concept. Just like every hole on a golf course, every blind retrieve has a fairway. Judges expect you to keep your dog within the fairway all the way to the bird. Why? Because a blind retrieve is a test of control, not a random run.

To determine the fairway for a blind retrieve, stand at the line, extend your right (or left) arm towards the bird with your fist up.

Position your second knuckle on the bird. Now raise your thumb and little fingers. The area between those raised digits marks the fairway for that particular blind.

Whenever your retriever strays from that fairway, blow the whistle and handle him back into it. If you allow him to run wild and handle him only when he reaches the approximate distance of the bird, you fool no one. You only demonstrate that you don't have the level of control over your dog that the particular test requires.

Further, you need to understand that there are times when your retriever will run a better blind if you give him a false line, that is, aim him a bit to the right or left of the true line to the bird. For example, in a strong crosswind, you should line your dog a little into the wind, because he will drift naturally with it as he runs. Similarly, if the line to the bird runs along the side of a hill, angle him slightly uphill, because he will drift naturally downhill. How far into the wind or up the hill? Depends on your dog. You are responsible for knowing how much he drifts and compensating accordingly.

However, angle him out of the fairway at your peril. Many judges will drop you automatically for this. I won't—as long as your

dog "bananas" back in on his own. If you guess wrong and have to handle him back into the fairway after aiming him out of it, I figure you haven't read the operator's manual on your particular dog, so I feel justified in dropping you. On the other hand, if he bananas nicely back somewhere near the bird, I will go into ecstasy at the teamwork and mutual

Perry Overstake locates the fairway in relation to the cone.

215

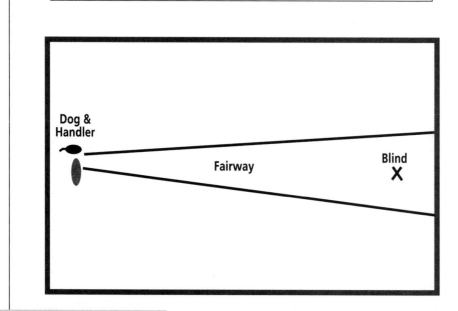

Dog & Handler

Fairway

Blind
X

FIG. 20: The fairway concept in blind retrieves
This diagram illustrates the "fairway" concept for blind retrieves. You should keep your dog in the fairway all the way to the bird. If he veers off out of it, stop him, and cast him back into the fairway. The blind retrieve is a test of control and teamwork. The handler who allows his dog to run wild outside the fairway demonstrates neither control nor teamwork.

understanding you have demonstrated. I will score you higher than the more mundane citizen who hacks and chops his dog down the middle of the fairway.

Your retriever has many little idiosyncrasies, and the better you understand them, the better you can handle him on a blind retrieve. For example, you should know how far he runs and which way he turns when you blow the stop whistle. That allows you to toot it so he stops where you want him to, or close to it. To be aware of this, you must study your dog in training.

You also need to know which way he turns when you send him back. He may always turn to your right. He may always turn to your left. He may turn left with a left-arm BACK and right with a right-arm BACK. That is ideal, of course, and some pros train their dogs that way, so they don't have to remember that little quirk for each dog in their strings. Most amateurs, who only have one or two dogs to worry about, can more easily remember this than train their dogs to turn with each arm.

If your dog always turns to your right on a BACK, you should compensate by stopping him differently on left and right OVERs. On a right OVER, you should stop him a bit early, because he will move farther to the right as he turns. On a left OVER, you should stop him late, because he will move back to the right as he turns. If he always turns to your left, you should reverse these handling procedures.

A Golden Retriever drives down the middle of the fairway in a water blind. Notice that if he goes out of the fairway on the left, he will be out of sight.

You also need to be aware of your dog's strengths and weaknesses, even the temporary ones. If he goes through a period in which his right-arm OVERs are weak, you should compensate by lining him so that you are less likely to have to give him that cast. Football coaches change their formations to suit the talents of their current crop of players. Golfers play around the clubs they aren't hitting well at the moment. Baseball pitchers use the pitches that they throw well on the day they pitch. You should do the same with your dog. You're there to help him, and that means you must think for him.

Naturally, you try to overcome his weaknesses in training, but in the real thing (whether that is a field trial, a hunting test, a working certificate test, or actual hunting), you should use your mind to make his job as easy as possible.

A Great Dog

1968 with Theresa

1969 Pheasant hunting

1984 16 years old

1972 At Cheney

1971 with Bob and Pat

1977 Show, Obedience, Field Trial Trophies

1973 in the Show Ring

Duncan Dell's MacDuff ** CD VC
February 7, 1968 – August 14, 1984

YOURS WILL BE A GREAT RETRIEVER ALL TOO SOON

Duffy is a great retriever. I remember the day he achieved that status. August 14, 1984.

Prior to that he had spent 16.5 years being a lot of other things. First, a sensitive, slow-maturing pup. Then, a gorgeous show-dog prospect with greater potential than I ever allowed him to realize. Next, a hard-running field trial dog. A hunting buddy that retrieved the first birds each of my two sons shot. An obedience trial dog. A Junior Showmanship dog for the Spencer girls. Then, when he became too old and feeble to do anything else, he spent four years as my fireside dog.

Finally (and sadly), he became a great retriever. A statesman is just a successful politician who has died, and a great retriever is just a working retriever that has died.

Every great dog is dead. Only then does the owner see the animal in the proper perspective.

On August 14, 1984 Duffy's positive attributes became unparalleled virtues. He was super-stylish back in the days when that was rare among goldens. And handle, my lord, how Duffy handled. Why, he relaxed when I said DEAD BIRD, as if to say, "Oh, boy, this one's your responsibility. You just direct me and I'll bring it back." He was beautiful. Conformation of a show dog, with the trophies and ribbons to prove it. Obedient, too, with a Companion Dog (CD) obedience trial title after his name. Most of all, he was a member of the family. During his last four years, when he lived in the house with me, he grew closer to me every day, followed me around everywhere, nudged my hand for attention when I sat down in my recliner.

Even his often-baffling training problems looked different on August 14, 1984. I have mentioned several of them in this book. He was terrified when I tried to teach him to heel as a pup. He wouldn't pick up a bird until he was a year old. He developed (thanks to a mistake of mine) a suction problem. He had to be handled too often on the third bird of a triple.

However, those problems had long been solved or accepted by August 14, 1984. They were learning experiences for both Duffy and me, and now for you. No frustration, no anxiety, remained. Only the satisfaction of working through or around them.

Even his lush show-dog coat took on a new light. Through all his active years, I hated it that I had to spend so much time de-burring him. Like it or not, I did it, in training as well as in hunting. I occasionally had to endure the ridicule of some macho-type whose attitude was, "The more pain and discomfort *my dog* can survive, the tougher *I am*." Now Duffy's gorgeous orange coat waves softly in the gentle breezes of my memory. "My lord," I think as I recall him, "he was a handsome animal."

Pictures of Duffy hang here and there throughout my house. One hangs on the wall in front of me as I write. As I look up at that picture, I can't remember a single thing he ever did that was less than brilliant. He gets better every day, and probably will until I join him in the heaven where dogs toot whistles and punish handlers for dumb mistakes.

Ditto for Duffy's nephew Brandy, who became a great dog just seven days before Duffy on August 7, 1984. He was unlike Duffy in everything but style. A hunting fool that only handled because he liked me. No show-dog was Brandy, and his sparse coat didn't adequately protect him in severe weather. Still, he sat shivering by the blind and dove gleefully into icy water time after time all day. Brandy was a dominant animal that ran every other dog on the place (including Uncle Duffy) like Hitler ran Germany. My son Bob, who trained Brandy for over two years, describes him simply: "Brandy took no prisoners." Still, since his death in 1984, he has become canonized in my mind.

The same for Misty the Weimaraner back in the 1950s. And for Cy, the German shorthair back in the 1960s. And. And. And.

However, when I look out in my runs right now, I see no legends. I see only dogs that I have to feed and clean up after every day. I see dogs that jump up on me at inopportune times—my wife has been telling me to stop this habit for years, but I like it most of the time. I see dogs with training problems that I haven't worked out yet.

Beaver, my 90 pound Chesapeake, is devoted to me (and I to him), but his heritage doesn't allow him to strive to please me like Duffy did. Beaver would rather fight and make up. I'm not a fighter, but he and I fight often, and I always win (by fair means or foul). Then, we always make up. That is so important to him. I mutter "Good boy" through gritted teeth quite often. Gradually Beaver is coming around, doing things more and more my way. Still, he relapses into problem behavior frequently, and we fight again.

Beaver is big, strong, and stylish. He ran five AKC junior stake hunting tests this past fall. He failed the first, then passed the next three. In the fifth, in which he could have finished his Junior Hunter title, he "stepped on" (marked perfectly) both land marks. Trouble was, he tried to eat the second one on the way in. Sure, the throwers apologized for throwing him a really bad pigeon, but he was out anyway. Now, I'm letting him forget that little incident before I start convincing him that birds, even "ripe" pigeons, are not for eating.

Beaver is not a perfect retriever in my mind at this moment. Still, in another fifteen years, I bet he will be. Brandy mashed a pigeon once. So did Misty.

Rhett, my young Golden, contrasts almost completely with Beaver. Rhett is cream colored, while Beaver is chocolate brown. Rhett is as small and soft as Beaver is big and tough. Rhett wants to please so desperately that it hurts. A harsh word from me paralyzes him. The only similarity between Rhett and Beaver is style. Both have plenty of it, as have all of my great and potentially great dogs.

Not everyone agrees with me, but style is my first priority in retrievers (as well as pointing dogs and flushing spaniels).

Rhett's coat is a burr magnet, more so even than Duffy's. I have already dug enough burrs from him to fill a pick-up bed, and he isn't two years old yet.

Rhett ran the same five AKC hunting tests and failed four of them, finding several creative ways to snatch failure out of the jaws of success. He will come around with more maturity and training. Duffy messed up many times in field trials. So did Brandy. Thus, I blindly believe that Rhett will become another legend.

Flicker, my huge (63 pound) young English springer spaniel, reminds me of Brandy, except that he is not a dominant dog. Wild, whole-hearted in everything he does, yet sensitive and eager to please.

Flicker's coat picks up more burrs than did Brandy's, but far fewer than did Duffy's. He also plucks many of them himself, as did Brandy. However, he collects grass-awns (which resemble foxtails) in his feet and sometimes in his eyes like no dog I have ever owned. In the grass-awn season, I have to go over him thoroughly every time I put him up after training.

A great flushing dog, Flicker retrieves well on land. In water, however, he sets a limit of about 60 yards on the distance he will swim. Beyond that he plays "Tony hit the ball; Tony chase the ball." Your experience will be no different. As long as your retriever lives— I hope that is a long time—he will be just a working retriever, a dog that retrieves a lot of birds for you, a dog you enjoy being with and training, but also a dog that requires a lot of work, a dog that baffles and frustrates you sometimes, a dog that advances through his training unevenly, a dog that has an occasional relapse that makes you wonder.

When your retriever baffles and frustrates you, take the long view. Think of his overall performance level. Think of how close the two of you have become. Think of all the things he has done right since you brought him home.

Most important, think of how trivial the particular problem will seem after you solve it. Review the other problems you have worked through successfully. None of them seem so serious now, do they? Neither will the current problem after you have overcome it.

"Insurmountable" problems? We all have them. I have force-broken many dogs of several breeds—pointing, spaniel, and retriever—over the past 35 years. Yet, I have never once completed that task without encountering a new "unsolvable" problem, a wall I couldn't see over or around. Every dog has done something no previous dog did, has resisted where no other dog resisted.

I have found that persistence overcomes most such problems. I sometimes back up a step or two and come at the problem area more cautiously, but more often I just keep working at it. Giving up doesn't solve anything.

However, if persistence doesn't solve a problem in a reasonable length of time, I follow the example of most amateur golfers. I take some "lessons" from a pro. I took Duffy's suction problem to Jim Robinson, Brandy's popping to D. L. Walters. If I have similar difficulties with any present or future dog, I will again go to a pro for assistance. So should you. Look on the pro as part of your retriever's support group, just as you do your veterinarian.

In training with several other people (as you should do), you cannot avoid comparing the dog's progress with that of the others. The trouble is, you will tend to compare your dog most often with any dog that is doing better, developing faster. That leads some into the trap of "competitive training," which induces them to rush their dogs faster than nature intended.

Whenever you feel you must bring your dog along faster than someone else in your group, ask yourself, "If I win this training session, what is the prize?" More often than not, it is a bewildered retriever.

Several years from now, when your dog has achieved great retriever status, you will forget all the mistakes he made during his life. However, you will remember—and magnify—every training error you made. The only blemishes on my memories of my great dogs are my personal errors.

I remember the times I pushed a dog too rapidly. This has delayed the training program every time, for I have always had to go

back a few spaces and start again. Even more, it has led me into punishing a dog unjustly. Every dog has a keen sense of justice which
shouldn't be violated. Fortunately, every dog also has a forgiving
heart, especially for the person he accepts as his master.

I remember the times I didn't properly analyze a problem. Like
when a Lab balked at the large dummies in force-breaking because
she had never seen one before. At first, I thought she was being
stubborn, so I applied more pressure.

I remember the times I have over-worked a dog. This is not a
common failing of mine, but I have done it. You know, just one
more test, one more rerun, and I think we will be getting somewhere. Now, just one more. And on. And on.

Most of all, I remember the times I punished in anger. A pro
once told me that the first couple or three strokes with a whip are
for the dog, but any additional strokes are for the trainer, indicating
he is out of control. I wish I could forget the extra strokes I have
occasionally inflicted. I also wish I could forget the look the dog
gave me as I did it.

Those are the kind of things you will wish you could forget one
day when you reminisce about your great retriever. Think about that
often as you take that young pup sitting there by your side through
his training.

One day he will only be a memory. Train him thoroughly, so he
will be a great memory. Train him compassionately, so you will have
nothing you would rather forget.

Index

A

Activities:
  Dog Shows: 219
  Field Trials: x, 52, 57, 61,
    71, 77, 91, 100, 103,
  131, 135, 146, 151, 152,
  153, 159-161, 162, 168,
    185, 191, 193, 195, 196,
  200, 212, 213,214, 217
  Herding Trials: 160
  Hunting Tests: x, 52, 57, 61,
    71, 77, 100, 103, 131,
    135, 146, 152, 153, 162,
    168-169, 185, 191, 193,
    195, 196, 200, 212, 213,
    214, 217,221, 222
  Obedience Trials: 39, 59, 63,
    219
  Working Certificate Tests: 2,
    52, 57, 131, 146, 152,
    195, 213, 217
Arm Signals (see also "Blind
    Retrieve—Casting): 6, 62,
    161, 165-169, 186-191,
    195, 209

B

Bank Running: 91, 148, 149,
    179, 211
Bare Ground: 8-9, 30, 77-79,
    80-84, 85, 86, 137-141,
    187-190, 194, 196-197
Baseball Casting Drills:
  General References: 162-
    163, 169, 186-187, 201
  Cone: 186-191
Birds:
  General References: ix, 6, 71,
    72, 80, 84-85, 96, 106,
    111, 123, 126, 127, 129,
    145, 157-159
  Doves: 158-159
  Pheasants: ix, 39, 72, 74, 76,
85, 127
  Pigeons: 72, 74, 84-85, 86,
    95, 101, 127, 221
  Quail: 37-38
  Ruffed Grouse: 2
  Waterfowl: ix, 1, 38, 51-52,
    72, 74, 85, 91, 103, 113-
    114, 127, 157

Blind Retrieve (Parts):
  Casting: 161-163, 184, 185,
  186-191, 201, 206
  Lining: 161-163, 171-179,
  184, 185, 191, 201, 206
  Stopping: 161-163, 180-186,
191, 201, 206
Blink, Blinking, Blinker: 108-
  111, 183
Bolting: 27
Books:
  "Charles Morgan on
  Retrievers": 104-105
  "Hunting Retrievers": 2
  "Retriever Training Tests": 2
  "Training Your Retriever":
  104, 186
Break, Breaking: 80-84, 137,
  145, 152, 154-155
Breeds:
  American Water Spaniel: 2, 4
  Boston Terrier: 69
  Brittany: 104
  Chesapeake: 2, 4, 23, 125,
  137, 170, 182, 221
  Curly-Coated Retriever: 2, 4
  English Springer Spaniel: 5, 222
  Flat-Coated Retriever: 2, 4,
  59, 63, 65, 72, 94-95,
  133, 134, 135, 153, 154
  Flushing Spaniels (All): 5, 9,
  104, 223
  German Shorthaired Pointer:
  104, 221
  German Wirehaired Pointer:
  104
  Golden Retriever: 2, 39, 51,
  77, 85, 89, 101, 108,
  109, 111, 113, 147, 153,
  182, 185, 221
  Irish Water Spaniel: 2, 4
  Labrador Retriever: 4, 23,
  27, 53, 106, 135
  Nova Scotia Duck Tolling
  Retriever: 2, 4
  Pointer: 37-38, 103-104
  Pointing Breeds (All): 8, 9,
  79,104, 223
  Vizsla: 104
  Weimaraner: 101, 104, 221
  Wirehaired Pointing Griffon:
  104

C
Clubs/Organizations:
  American Kennel Club
  (AKC): 100
  Curly-Coated Retriever Club
  of America (CCRCA): xiv
  Dog Writers Association of
  America (DWAA): xiv
  Field Trial Clubs (in general):
2, 8, 9-10
  Flat-Coated Retriever Society
of America (FCRSA): xiv
  Golden Retriever Club of
  America (GRCA): xiv
  Golden Retriever Club of
  Canada (GRCC): xiv
  Hunting Test Clubs
  (in general): 2, 8
  Jayhawk Retriever Club
  (JRC): 86
  North American Hunting
  Retriever Association

(NAHRA): 100
Local Breed Clubs
(in general): 2
United Kennel Club (UKC): 100
Hunting Retriever Club
(HRC): 100
Commands, Verbal:
Back!: 19, 20, 29, 158, 167-
168, 187-191, 205, 208,
215, 216
Blind Retrieve Sequence:
(See "Dead Bird . . . .")
Come, Come-In: 19, 39, 40,
66-68, 105, 167-168
Dead Bird . . . Line . . .
Back!: 158, 164-165, 172-
179, 201, 207, 219
Down!: 19, 39, 40, 68-69
Dog's Name (as a
command): 29
Fetch!: 19, 29, 102, 103,
109-127, 141
Give!: 19, 102, 103, 109-127
Heel!: 19, 39, 40, 51-61, 62,
67, 68, 69, 82, 105, 145,
155,
Hush!: 19, 21-23, 24
Kennel!: 19, 39, 40, 48-51
No!: 19, 20, 21, 24, 40, 50,
62, 64, 82, 145, 164-165,
176, 177, 178, 206, 207,
210
Over!: 19, 158, 167-168,
184, 186-191, 205, 216
Release!: 19, 39, 40, 46-51,66
Sit!: 19, 20, 39, 40, 46-48,
51, 62, 105, 116, 141,
155, 176, 180-186, 187

Stay!: 19, 20, 39, 40, 59, 60,
62-66, 67, 68, 69, 81-82,
105, 116, 139, 141, 154,
155, 176, 187
Commands, Whistle:
General References: 6, 165-
166, 195
Come-In!: 30, 66, 67, 68,
75, 187-191
Sit! (Or Stop!): 61, 67, 161,
180-186
Conditioning (Process): x-xi,
53-55, 200
Conditions (Environmental):
Cover (on land): 9, 30, 71,
80, 85-88, 142-146, 190-
191, 198-199
Cover (in water): 9, 90-93,
190-191, 198-199
Terrain: 86, 144, 190-191
Wind: 86, 88, 139-140, 144,
148, 162, 188, 190-191,
197, 215

D

Delivery to Hand: 89, 100-101,
136
Dogs (mentioned by name):
Beaver (Chesapeake): 17, 23,
125, 137, 170, 171, 182,
221
Belle (Golden): xii, 147, 187
Brandy (Golden): xii, 19,
184, 185, 220-221, 222
Cindy (Golden): 89-90
Cy (German Shorthair): 221

Deuce (Golden): 49, 110-111, 114-115, 118-119, 121, 124-125, 126

Duffy (Golden): xii, 19, 51-53, 55, 57-58, 84, 100-101, 158-159, 185, 193, 204, 219-224

Flicker (English Springer): 5, 222

Fortune (Flat-Coat): 59, 63, 65, 72, 94-95, 134, 153, 154

Hustler (Golden): 77, 84

Jigger (Pointer): 103

Katie (Labrador): 23, 53, 55, 126-127

Mickey (Golden): 105, 185

Misty (Weimaraner): 69, 76, 101-102, 103, 122, 221

Pepper (Labrador): 106

Pirate (Golden): 185

Rhett (Golden): 2, 182, 221-222

Rumrunner's B&B (Golden): 90

Scandal (Flat-Coat): 133, 134, 135

Scrappy (Boston Terrier): 69

Summer (Golden): 55, 81, 82, 94-95, 153, 154

Tina (Golden): 108, 113-114

E

Equipment:
Belt Cord: 72, 73, 80-84, 95, 136, 145, 154, 194, 198
Boat: 34, 48, 194, 199

Buck (Force-Breaking): 106-127

Blank Pistol: 72, 73, 74, 79-80, 96, 137

Collar (in general): 24, 42-44, 48, 106

Collar, Chain Training: 18, 20, 42-44, 47, 51-61, 107, 112

Collar, Choke: 42

Collar, Electronic: ix, 212

Collar, Strap: 18, 19, 42, 47

Cone (traffic): 169-170, 172-179, 187-191, 207, 209

Decoys: 2, 53, 71, 93-96, 149, 159

Duck Call: 96

Dummies (retrieving): 8-9, 18, 20, 24-30, 72-96, 111, 137, 139, 140, 174-179, 186-191

Flexi-Lead: 20

Gloves: 19

Jacket (white): 168-169

Lanyard: 45-46, 73

Lead (leash): 18, 20, 27, 28, 44, 47-48, 51, 53-61, 64, 65, 66, 93, 106, 111, 112, 116, 120

Rope: 18-19, 84-85, 90

Shotgun: 6, 53, 71, 80, 96, 135, 152, 193, 194

Stakes (wooden): 169, 178-179

Stool: 6, 135, 194

Vest: 79

Whistle: 45-46, 73

F

Fairway (in blind retrieves):
 214-217
Fall(s):
 Angle of: 76, 196-197, 198
 Area of: 144
 Diversion Bird: 129, 130, 136,
  139, 145, 146, 194, 199
 Length of: 77-79, 86, 90, 92,
  130, 138, 143, 196-197,
  198, 199
 Memory Bird: 129, 130, 136,
  137, 139, 142, 145, 146,
  147, 194, 199
 Sequence of: 5, 129, 138,
  143, 144, 197, 198
Food (as reward): 27
Force-Breaking: xiv, 5, 10, 30,
 89, 99-127, 132, 223
Force Methods:
 Choke: 118
 Ear Pinch: 117
 Lip Pinch: 117
 Paw Squeeze: 118

G

Gun: (see also "Thrower"):
 General References: 85
 Hidden Gun: 77, 96, 135,
  151-152, 198
 Retiring Gun: 77, 150, 151-
  152, 198
Gun-Proofing: 71, 79-80, 85

H

Handling on a Mark: 195-196,
 213-214
Handling Techniques: 6-7, 55-
 69, 71-72, 132-137, 164-
 169, 194-196, 213-217
Hard-Mouth: 101-102
Head-Swinging: 146
Hell Week (Force-Breaking): xiv,
 100, 105
Honoring: 81, 152-155

K

K.I.S.S. (Keep It Simple, Stupid!):
 6, 72, 95, 133, 194

L

Lair: xiii, 24, 28, 75

M

Magazines:
 Gun Dog: xii, xiv
 Retriever International: xiv
Marking: 129. 142
Memory: 129, 142, 145, 147, 198

O

Obedience: 3-5, 37-69, 96, 105,
 106

P

Pattern Blinds:
General References: 162, 164, 172-173, 184
Cone: 172-179, 206-2-7, 209
Floating Dummy: 172, 179
Mowed Path: 172-173
Sight Blind: 172-173
Persons (mentioned by name):
Bunn, Carrell: xiv
Carlisle, Jay: 161
Corbin, Marilyn: 54, 72, 81, 82, 94-95, 153, 154
Driskill, Omar: 96-97
Elliott, Dave: 159-161
Foote, Marianne: xiv
Free, James Lamb: 104, 186
Gallagher, Mary Jo: 58, 59, 63, 65, 72, 94-95, 134, 153, 154
Gallagher, Mike: 58, 133, 134, 135
Kincaid, Darrell: xii, 45, 214
Morgan, Charles: 104-105
Overstake, Perry: 215
Patton Margaret: 172
Robinson, Jim: 223
Sanborn, David: 103-104, 118
Walters, D.L.: ix, 184, 223
Picture (Blind Retrieve Concept): xiii, 164, 171-172, 205, 207
Pig, Piggy: 183, 184
P.I.L. (Poor Initial Line): 205, 207-208
Place Consciousness: 109, 130, 141, 207, 208

Play Retrieving: 23-29, 71, 75
Pop, Popping: 184, 207, 209-210, 223

R

Rapport: xi-xii
Refusal:
Cast: 208
To Go: 145, 207-210
Water: 89, 91, 147, 149
Whistle: 208
Rehearsing: 142, 143, 146, 150, 198
Rerun: 86, 140, 141, 142-143, 150, 151, 189, 191, 198, 205, 208
Retrieve Types
Blind: xi, xiii, 3, 5, 6, 7, 8, 11, 29, 86, 106, 152, 157-191, 199-212
Marked (general references): xi, 3, 5, 6, 29, 183, 211
Marked (single): xiii, 5, 8, 10, 71-96, 129, 132, 146, 210
Marked (multiple): xiii, 5, 8, 11, 84, 86, 106, 129-155, 161, 193-199, 212-214
Mixed: 199-200, 204
Retrieving Instinct: 23-24
Rumrunner Goldens: 8, 19, 77

S

Salting: 86-87, 142, 143, 150, 198
Selecting: 131, 135, 195, 212-213

Steadiness, Steadying: 74, 80-84,
  96, 132
Stickiness: 102-103
Style: xv, 4, 219-222
Suction: 199-200, 211, 223
Switching: 5; 130-131, 135, 137,
  139-140, 141, 143, 144,
  147, 152, 197, 198

T

Thrower (see also "Gun"): 7, 71,
  74-77, 79-80, 88, 89, 91,
  95, 133, 135, 136, 138,
  144-145, 204
Trainers:
  Amateur: ix-xiv, 105, 196
  Professional: ix-xiv, 11-12, 26,
  105, 145, 149, 209-210,
  223

Training Group: 7-8
Transitional Drill:
  Dummy String: 202-207, 211
  Thrown Blind: 202, 204-207,
  211
Trial-and-Error: xi, 8, 198
Trial-and-Success: xi, 8, 30, 198
Tone of Voice: 41-42

V

Veterinarian: 15, 223

W

Water-Beating: 30, 34-35, 90
Water Forcing: 91, 149, 212
Water Work: 30-35, 88-96, 146-
  151, 178-179, 191, 198-
  199, 211-212, 222